PRAISE FOR *STRAY*

"*Stray* is a raw-boned beauty of a story, as fierce and brave as the author herself."

— Alexandra Styron, author of *Reading My Father: A Memoir*

"A sharply etched portrait of working-class teenage life in small-town Canada, Tanya Marquardt's *Stray* is an engrossing coming-of-age story that is moving, funny, and heartbreaking. Unafraid to travel to dark places, Tanya shows a tenderness, innocence, and wonder that makes us nod in recognition at what it is to leave childhood behind and enter the adult world. The prose is sparse, direct, and elegant. I couldn't put it down, and I read it in one day."

— Carmen Aguirre, author of *Something Fierce: Memoirs of a Revolutionary Daughter*

STRAY

MEMOIR OF A RUNAWAY

TANYA MARQUARDT

Little
a

Published by Little A, New York
www.apub.com

Amazon, the Amazon logo, and Little A are trademarks of Amazon.com, Inc., or its
affiliates.

ISBN-13: 9781503949164 (hardcover)
ISBN-10: 1503949168 (hardcover)
ISBN-13: 9781503949140 (paperback)
ISBN-10: 1503949141 (paperback)

Cover design by Isaac Tobin

Printed in the United States of America

First edition

For Mr. Walecki

AUTHOR'S NOTE

This is a memoir, meaning that it is sourced from my memories, diaries, letters, and recollections. Dialogue is reconstructed, and some names and identifying features have been changed to provide anonymity.

ONE

Running

Disappearance

When I left, I took everything with me.

It was November 1, 1995. My sixteenth birthday. I leapt off the bus, my backpack and schoolbooks rattling against my ribcage, pounding in rhythm to my feet galloping up the driveway. My sneakers slid along the gravel as I swerved, taking a hard left. I only had forty-five minutes before Mom came home from work. There was a lot to pack.

I kicked open the door of Don's redbrick house and ran up the steps that led to the kitchen. Under the sink, behind the Ajax and the dishwashing detergent, there were two large garbage bags. I pulled them out, shoved them into the back pocket of my blue jeans, slid across the linoleum floor *Dukes of Hazzard* style, and scrambled down the hallway to my bedroom.

I was blind to everything but hatred. I hated Mom and decided I would erase myself from her life, punishing her for moving us to Port Alberni, a small town in the middle of nowhere, where we lived with her boyfriend, Don, and his four children.

My room in Don's house was half-finished. I had written on the exposed drywall with blue ink and black marker, mostly Shakespeare quotes, poetry about death, and the lyrics to Led Zeppelin's "Tangerine." One morning I woke up to find Mom sitting next to me, scanning the fresh pen marks on my wall.

"Don't get used to this, Tanya. Don is going to be painting this wall any day now. Besides, girls shouldn't be writing things like this," she said, leaning in to read one of my poems.

Mom never asked to see my poems, didn't tack them to the fridge or put them on display. She had pictures of Don's kids on the fridge, why not one of my strange poems? Of course, Mom had told me, her words echoing in the air, *Girls shouldn't be writing things like this.* She was worried what Don or his family would think of me and, more importantly, of her. Still, I waited for a response, wanting to see a look of recognition on her face, a hint of acceptance.

Her eyes widened.

"'The wolves listen to us howling'? 'We will become ash'? 'They will walk over us'? This is disturbing."

I loved to write, and Mom's rejection of such a raw and exposed part of me was worse than if she'd slapped me, and like fuel to a fire, it caused a rage that burned inside my belly.

She stared at the poem, her eyes glazing over. There had always been limits to Mom's ability to engage. Day-to-day errands like grocery shopping were Mom's strong suit, zipping through aisles, tossing bread and soap in our cart while simultaneously price-checking ground beef. But when confronted with a need that contradicted hers, or with emotional turmoil that she couldn't control, she shut off. One minute we would be talking about my schoolwork in the kitchen, her face animated, her hands gesticulating. And then I might bring up Dad, or how my brother Kyle wasn't adjusting to school postdivorce, and like a TV shutting off in slow motion, her jaw would go slack and whatever we were saying or doing just didn't register.

I shook off the memory by opening my closet to scoop all my clothes off the rack, heave them onto my bed, and survey the mess. Pairs of extralong bell-bottoms with ripped knees lay in a heap alongside secondhand peasant shirts, a coveted knee-length corduroy jacket that dyed patches of my T-shirts orange when it rained, and old-man pants three sizes too big for my six-foot-tall, one-hundred-and-fifteen-pound frame. I stuffed the wire hangers into a box, sandwiched the clothes into a garbage bag and chucked it aside without bothering to tie it shut. Socks and underwear, all cheap, all white, were emptied from my dresser and into the second garbage bag. Shoes—men's nine or ten because Mom couldn't find cheap shoes in a women's twelve—went into a cardboard box. Notebooks and textbooks were shoved into a decaying blue backpack with a missing strap and a broken zipper. The leather case that held my cassette tapes was hurled on top of the pile. The copy of Shakespeare's sonnets, *Hamlet*, and *Richard III*, for my theater class, went into a cardboard box along with my toothbrush, toothpaste, tampons, and shampoo. I crumpled up the sheets, coverlet, pillows, and duvet and threw them onto the pile.

After looking around the room, I felt sure I had gotten everything. Then I remembered. I reached under my bed where there were two leather-bound journals that had gold lettering on the front covers and that fastened with a flimsy lock. I read the lettering out loud to myself and gingerly placed the books into my backpack.

Diary.

I would need to write.

I called a cab, stacked my stuff outside, and stood by the front door, my bare hands freezing as I lit a cigarette, my lungs filling with smoke.

"Come on, come on," I whispered to myself.

My heart was beating against the inside of my ribcage, my breathing labored from packing my life into two garbage bags, a school backpack, and a cardboard box.

I heard the slow sound of tire on gravel coming up the driveway.

Is it Mom? I thought, clutching at the front of my jacket.

I started to twitch in anticipation.

What would Mom do? I wondered. Would she yell at me, demand I come back into the house? Would she slam her car door shut, stare at me in disbelief? Would she beg me to stay?

I couldn't be sure. I had played the possible scenarios in my head, imagining myself spitting on the ground Mom walked on, pulling away before stepping into the cab, or waiting until the middle of the night and climbing out my window to leave with only the clothes on my back. But standing there, I knew. If Mom turned the corner I would fall into a heap on the ground. I would wail, and when she reached out to touch me, I would recoil and she would be forced to move all my stuff inside while I chain-smoked myself into a nonresponsive state. I didn't want to leave her. I wanted it to be her. I wanted her to stop me.

The car rounded the corner, a yellow cab that pulled into the driveway and idled. The driver, an older man with tanned, leathery skin, a beer belly, and a Toronto Blue Jays baseball cap, unrolled the driver's side window and stuck his head out.

"Got lost," he said matter-of-factly.

There wasn't any more time. I picked up the bags, the pillows, and the backpack and teetered over to the cab. The cabbie popped the trunk but didn't offer to help, and I saw the confusion on his face as I passed by the window, probably wondering where a teenager would be going with unwrapped bedsheets and a cardboard box filled with shampoo and wire hangers. I shoved the stuff into the trunk and climbed in.

"Corner of Third and Argyle," I said, trying to use my adult voice.

The cabbie and I looked at each other in the rearview mirror, but he said nothing. As the cab picked up speed, I closed my eyes to avoid watching Don's house fade from sight.

Drive

The last time our family was together—Mom, Dad, Kyle, Jack, and me—was in Nelson, British Columbia. We moved there in 1990, after my youngest brother, Jack, was born. That was where Dad stopped drinking for a year, a promise he made to us after he had been arrested for drunk driving, and for twelve straight months he behaved like the perfect father—got up on Saturday mornings, took Kyle and Jack to the park, carved the ham at dinner, kissed my mother on Sundays. The majority of our childhood photos from this year exist because Dad took them, photos of my nine-year-old brother Kyle waddling through a pond, or baby Jack wrapped in a towel on his first birthday or dressed as a clown for his first Halloween.

Mom sang Dolly Parton songs in the kitchen, sometimes humming and sometimes belting them out off-key, her tall frame and thin fingers doing quick work while her soft black curls brushed against her pale skin and bright-green eyes. "Jolene" and "Coat of Many Colors" underscored the packing of our school lunches, with me looking on in awe, wondering why Mom had black hair while mine was blonde, like Dolly's. Mom had a system where she laid out six pieces of white bread on the counter, placed bologna and cheese slices on top of the bread, and then put the sandwiches together before stuffing chocolate pudding, a plastic spoon, and carrots into the brown paper bags. She kept the brown paper bags in the cupboard near the stove, along with her "no more Jack" pills.

"We love Jack, but we don't want no more of 'em," she would joke before throwing the pink dot into her mouth, downing water like a tequila shot and shutting off for a moment as she swallowed, looking off into the horizon outside the kitchen window.

Nelson filled my family with an unparalleled sense of salvation, a sense that we had finally done something right. We banded together for the first time ever in the pursuit of this rightness—this dream of rightness. With a manic kind of joy, an overwhelmingly fragile belief that we could simply erase our pasts as if nothing had ever happened in the history of our family, we blotted out ten years and in its place, we moved into a house with an evergreen terrace and gleaming white walls, the beginning of a strange and intoxicating dream.

I have a picture of me standing beside a bookshelf in Dad's office filled with construction manuals and Time-Life condensed novels that my mother bought and put on the bookshelves to give the impression that Dad read in his office. The light in the photo is orange and fading and you can tell it's near dusk. I am looking over my shoulder, tanned and tall and lean, feigning confidence. An awkward girl of twelve, I judged myself harshly, sure that people were staring at the rail-thin arms dangling at my sides, my concave chest, and my stick-figure legs.

The end of our family grew out of this beginning. When we arrived, no one knew where we had come from. They didn't know that we came from Red Deer, Alberta, or that we had lived in that city for less than eight months. They didn't see how shoddily we had packed our boxes, shoving our things into whatever cardboard box we could in less than two days after my father's boss scammed us out of thousands of dollars and disappeared. They didn't know that this wasn't the first time my father had been scammed, or that he had scammed other people out of their money. They didn't know that my father drank vodka every night until he was incoherent, or that he couldn't cross the American border because of a possession conviction. They didn't know that my mother and I spent many evenings cleaning up beer bottles and broken glass, and they didn't know that we could be berated, hugged, scolded, slapped, demeaned, or put into servitude at the whim of Dad, the traveling salesman and cocaine addict. And for that first year, our neighbors thought that we were the nice new family that lived across the street, down the lane, over on the next block, next door, in the house near the lake on Nelson Avenue.

As a traveling vacuum cleaner salesman, Dad was gone two or three weeks every month, and when he was home he would practice his routines on us, watch motivational videos, go to team meetings, and read pamphlets, refining the subtle art of salesmanship. His voice was practiced and well sung, a salesman's pitch and timbre, crafty, fast-paced, and witty, donning all the characters, all the clichés. Dad knew how to flirt with lonely housewives and elderly ladies, how to make men feel guilty for not providing for their children. He'd get into their house, sprinkle dirt onto their carpet, vacuum the floors clean, and then, when they were at his mercy, pull back their comforter and vacuum the bedsheets to show them how dirty they were. This was the ultimate tactic, playing on human shame and secrecy. He was saying, *I know you. I'm the stranger that knows all about your dirty bedsheets.*

"And when's the last time you thought about your carpets, Mrs. Jones? I bet you don't give them much thought with the young ones running around. What do these carpets hide? A bit of dirt? A little dust? I want to show you what they are really hiding, what your children are playing on. There's a new study, just out, in *Scientific American*—do you read *Scientific American*? It's about germs, Mrs. Jones. Germs. We've done independent studies, and that is what's in these carpets. With our air-filtration system you can reduce the amount of germs, as well as the pollen, the dust, the dirt. Did you know that 90 percent of the air around us is full of dead human skin? It clings to our couches, our sheets, our carpets. Human skin. Do you have allergies, Mrs. Jones? Did you know that overexposure to dust, skin, and hair left behind by our pets and whatever animals we come into contact with can cause premature allergic reactions, especially in children?" And on and on.

In Regina a few years before, he spent our rent money on drugs, and I watched my mother howl on the couch with my aunt. He had been gone for over a month, and there had been no warning, no phone calls. Mom found out because our rent check bounced. She was certain we'd be evicted, and borrowed money from her sister until Dad arrived over a week later, with his tie half-done and stained slacks. He looked like a half-dead thing, a thing that wasn't afraid to let us starve.

I cannot reconcile myself with the memory of this addict father and the one who painstakingly built me a bedroom in the basement of our house in Nelson and installed a door for me made of dusted glass. After Dad was finished, he bought me a desk to put in the corner, with a map of the world laminated on it. I was given spiral-bound notebooks, and I wrote in them like I was trying to win a race, rocking back and forth, knocking my knees against the underside of my desk, an attempt to shake the words out through my hands with the same voracity with which they were pounding around inside my head.

All it took were these small acts of kindness for me to forgive him. I held him to a lower standard, expected much less from him because he demanded that we accept his unpredictability. And I wanted him to love me because I thought that he didn't love me the way he loved my brothers. On weeknights he made me sit at his feet and prepare peanut butter crackers for him. He yelled at me to equally spread the peanut butter on all four sides while Kyle and Jack lay in his arms. The three of them sat together for hours. I watched them watch movies from where I sat on the floor, totally separate, completely shut out.

After a year of sobriety, Dad started drinking again. He gave us no excuses and no end date. One day he was sober and the next day he was drinking. Dad would make the front-seat passenger mix his drinks. Three parts vodka to one part Coca-Cola. From early childhood I learned how to hide booze from cops, ferry attendants, waitresses, res-taurant owners, other drivers, my mother, his customers, my grandpar-ents, and my teachers. I knew that people thought a safe driver was a sober driver, but I thought it was safer to drive with a drunk when they were drunk and not when they were trying to get sober. I knew that if you were in a car with a drunk, you had to be nice, and you couldn't get angry about the fact that they were drunk. It was best to speak slowly. You had to be nice—very, very nice—and coax them, gently, into the rest area, then hope they would lull themselves to sleep in the backseat of the car, while you poured out their booze.

During long car trips, we would watch Dad get drunk all day, and then later, we would watch him pass out. As he slipped into oblivion the space that we'd been holding around him all day fell away like a security blanket. We were the thick air that warmed my father as he maneuvered us across the country.

After several weeks of drinking, Dad got into a car accident, and when he failed a breathalyzer, his license was revoked for six months. He was also sentenced to eight consecutive weekends in jail, three days and two nights in solitary confinement. He was allowed a deck of cards and two packs of cigarettes. On Fridays I would watch him walk into the police station, no cuffs or officers waiting, and for a split second it seemed like he was going to visit a relative or have a weird adult slumber party. But then I would see his shoulders, heavy and slumped over, and realize I was lying to myself. I imagined him alone with no one to talk to, and couldn't think of a worse punishment than having to sit in a concrete room with no light and no people. Every Sunday evening we would park in front of the police station and wait for him to walk through the front doors, haggard and worn out as he climbed into the car.

One Friday my brothers and I had said our goodbyes and were waiting for Mom and Dad to finish talking. Mom was clinging to her purse, holding it with her arms crossed around her belly, nodding, *Yes,*

yes, ah-ha, yes. They looked at one another like something was supposed to happen but neither of them knew what. Then, Dad grabbed Mom, thrust her into his face, and kissed her like he was trying to inhale her. Stunned, Mom dropped her long arms to her sides and went limp. She did not put her arms around him. When he stopped Mom took a half step backward and nodded, a final dazed *yes.* She looked like a lean, slender horse, something out of *Black Beauty,* but weak, as if her legs were about to buckle and she might faint. Then Dad went inside the police station, where there was a small holding cell in the back for him to stay in. Mom paused to get her bearings, bracing her bony arm against the hood of the car, and then got in.

I thought she might say something, but instead we all sat and watched the door to the police station swing shut, its glass shimmering in the early evening light. Once we were certain that Dad was inside, Mom turned on the ignition and we drove away. We were all confused and relieved by Dad's incarceration. I didn't want him to suffer, but it felt good when he was gone for the weekend. I could breathe, I slept better, Mom would order in, and we could all lounge around. I thought I should miss him. But I didn't.

A few weeks after Dad got out of jail, he was drinking at the dinner table when Mom asked him to slow down a little. That's when he stood up, hunched over, and threw our VCR out the back door and down the stairs. Most of the parts went outside, and no one got cut. But hot air poured into the house through the back door, and pieces shattered as they flew across the driveway into the alley. In my memory it was a soundless moment, Dad grotesque and graceful, a bull in a china shop, suspended and dancing.

The first time I smoked, I stole a pack of Dad's cigarettes from inside the fridge door, where he kept a carton of them next to the butter, and went down to the basement. The plastic around the soft pack stuck to my fingers and made a crinkling sound as I unwrapped it. As I pulled back the silver foil a smell hit me, something familiar, sage mixed with ash and leather. There were twenty cigarettes hiding underneath the silver wrapping, and I squeezed one of the filters to pull one away from the others. It felt like a sponge. I wondered if Dad had the same thought every time he took one of his cigarettes, tapping it on the table three times before putting it in his mouth. I cupped the smoke in my hands like an alien artifact, rolling it over to search for a secret of Dad's that might be revealed along the cigarette's perforated tip. It was a daily punishment, watching him ingest poison after poison, not knowing how to make him stop smoking, stop drinking. Which was why I had the cigarette in my hands. I thought that if I smoked and if he saw me smoking, I would gain his power and the guilt would pass from me to him.

After only one puff, I was transfixed, the smoke rings wafting around my head like an embrace.

That summer I met Jeff Miller, one of my father's friends. He had long, dark hair, wore acid-wash jeans, and was always at our weekend BBQs. Jeff and Dad would stay up late on Fridays, smoke billowing outside, hollering at each other while downing beers and flipping steaks.

Jeff was up watching TV and drinking alone when he caught me sneaking into the house after smoking a midnight cigarette a few blocks away, by Kootenay Lake. Instead of chiding me or waking my father, he laughed about the whole thing, and then I laughed about the whole thing, and we sat together in the basement and watched TV while chatting and smoking cigarettes.

It was getting late when Jeff brought up his ex-girlfriends and how lonely he was. He came to sit beside me on the couch. I didn't say anything but I knew this kind of conversation wasn't normal. My body stiffened as Jeff reached for my hands, and I remember him rubbing them, almost chafing them.

"How old are you?" he asked me.

"Twelve."

"Twelve. Wow. Twelve. You are so much older than twelve. Twelve is just a number," Jeff said, rubbing my hands harder than ever. "It's like I can really talk with you, it's like you're really listening."

Jeff was looking into my eyes, searching for mutual desire.

My blood felt ice cold. I was shivering but my mind was completely empty, watching Jeff as if he were in the distance.

"Do you want a whiskey?" Jeff offered, pouring himself another glass.

"No, thanks," I said.

Then he excused himself "for just a second," to go to the bathroom.

As soon as he left I dashed into my room, which didn't have a door because Dad was in the middle of renovations. I turned out the lights, got under the covers with all my clothes still on, and listened to my measured breathing. Even with my eyes shut in the semidarkness, I could see the light emanating from under the bathroom door.

I heard the click of the bathroom light turn off and the door creak open. Jeff staggered toward the living room. There was a long silence. I could feel him thinking, wondering where I was. Then I heard his footsteps in the hallway, followed by another silence. More thinking. I heard his footsteps make their way to the doorway of my room. I felt like I could cut the silence, thick slabs of it in the space between him and me. Jeff's eyes were on me until I couldn't handle it anymore. I faked waking up, as if I had no idea he had been looming, backlit from the hanging bulb in the hallway.

"Going to sleep?" he asked.

"I'm tired," I said.

"Oh." A slight pause. "G'night then?"

"Good night."

I lay down and shut my eyes tightly, pretending that I was in a deep sleep, not saying anything. Jeff stared at me for a long while before stumbling back into the living room. I lay awake, counting the space between my breaths, listening for his footsteps for the rest of the night.

After that first year in Nelson, Mom started hiding clothes in my closet—pencil skirts, floral-patterned shirts, and women's jackets with oversized shoulder pads. She would try them on in my room.

"How do I look?" she would ask.

I had only ever seen her in T-shirts and jeans, and her canary-yellow blazer made her look like a child trying on her mother's clothes, her skinny frame more like a coat hanger than a woman's body, hidden under the broad shoulders and hanging fabric.

"You look great," I would lie. "The color suits you."

Mom would press the jacket with her hand, as if it were some kind of precious cargo.

"We're just going to keep this between you and me," Mom would say, shoving a bag full of pastel work shirts behind my blue jeans.

Soon after, Mom got a job as an accountant for a trucking company after years of being a housewife. Dad didn't like it and accused Mom of stealing his money to buy clothes. He saw her spending as a waste of time, especially for a job that he called "temporary."

One night, not long after Mom started working, Dad came home in a rage and started ripping pillows from the couch.

"Fuck, fuck, fuck," he snarled.

He fell into the kitchen and pulled knives and plates out of the cupboards.

Mom, Jack, Kyle, and I ran upstairs and hid in Mom's closet, squatting in the back where there was no light.

Kyle was shivering, and Jack kept asking, "Why is Daddy mad?"

"Shh, shh, quiet, quiet," Mom said.

We listened as Dad dragged the fridge across the floor, pushed it over, and *smash,* all the glass jars fell out and broke as they rolled down the basement stairs. Dad yelled and we heard him grab the electric stove and try to pry it from the wall. Dad pounded it with his fists until yelps of pain began to mix with his yelling. We listened until the pounding stopped, and then he was frantic and panting, talking to himself in drunken gibberish until he was sobbing and pleading, *please please please please,* over and over again. That slowly faded, and after a long while, all we could hear was silence.

We sat in the stillness until Mom felt it was safe. She inched herself along the closet wall to the door handle.

"Stay here," she whispered to us, standing up onto the carpeted floor.

There was no way to know what was going to happen, but the back of my head hurt from pressing it against the hard wall. I was trying to become the wall, shape-shift into shoes and dresses and anything else that was in that closet. I couldn't feel my breath in my body, and I didn't want to. As long as Dad didn't know where we were, we might be safe. We were all motionless, Kyle and Jack in the far corner of the closet behind the clothes where even I couldn't see them.

Eventually Mom came back into the room. The closet door opened slowly, gently. Her hair was glowing from the lamplight behind her, her face obscured, and the scent of her perfume, a strong lilac, floated in toward me, relief and recognition.

"It's okay now," she said.

She gathered Kyle and Jack in her arms. They barely moved—their bodies had shut down, asleep from fear. Mom took both of them to bed. I was alone, but it felt safer than being outside of the closet.

Then Mom came back.

"I have to take Dad to the hospital. Go downstairs and clean while I'm gone. Just clean it up, and be careful of the glass."

I waited until I heard the car pull out of the driveway and tiptoed down the staircase. The first thing I saw was the oven in the middle of the kitchen, blocking my way to the living room. It had come dangerously close to being pulled away from the gas pipe that secured it to the wall. Glasses and plates covered the linoleum floor, and the fridge lay open on its side, its bright light flashing like a neon sign directly into my face. I had never seen anything like it before. It was like a murder scene without a body, a break and enter but by someone I knew. Not knowing where to start, I bent over and started picking up glass shards. My big toe grazed a broken tumbler before I remembered that I was barefoot and retreated to the hall closet to get the broom. I swept up most of the glass and picked up the rest, putting any unbroken dishes into the sink to rinse them off before putting them into the dishwasher. I had a feeling of wanting to vomit, but I didn't throw up and I didn't cry and my hands didn't tremble. My world became my task, and proving that I was strong enough to clean up the mess. I moved the fridge back by myself by bracing it against the outside of my thigh and squeezing my fingers underneath it, heaving it to standing as the sandwich meat and the pickle jars rolled out onto the floor. In a way, it was like any other day, the slow buzzing anxiety ever present to the point of numbing me.

Mom and I moved the stove after they came back from the hospital. Dad had immediately gone upstairs to pass out. Both of us were barely able to match the strength it took for Dad to yank it from the wall, but we shimmied it back into place. I didn't see him until later that night, when I saw that his pinky fingers were in plaster casts. We never talked about how he broke them. Instead, I made jokes about it. By the next day, I was doing impressions of Dad trying to talk to us while gesticulating with two broken fingers, all of us laughing until we were crying.

"That's exactly what he looks like, Tanya," Mom would say. "You're so funny."

Dad never paid me much attention, opting to spend lucid hours making forts in the living room with Kyle and Jack, but when Mom told him that she wanted a divorce, that all changed.

Dad started taking me to the movies, for walks, for long car rides. He bought me A&W Root Beer and cheeseburgers, and he started giving me cigarettes and buying me my own packs. He gave me a tarot deck and took my brothers and me to visit my grandparents whenever we felt like it.

And I fell for it. Genuinely believing that Dad was making up for lost time, I began to be fiercely loyal to him, leaving Mom at home to fend for herself on weekends while the rest of us went on day-long adventures to the mall, chuckling under my breath when he put her down in front of us.

Dad told Kyle and me things we didn't know, starting with "all the horrible things Mom said" about us. How she didn't love Kyle, she had told my dad once, and now Dad felt it was his duty to sit Kyle down and tell him what Mom said, especially since Mom was trying to take us away from Dad. He also told us how Mom was working because she hated being a mother and taking care of us, how she had stolen Dad's money to buy clothes instead of buying us food and wait a minute, wasn't Jack hungry the other day? What kind of mother would starve her child?

He would press us to "tell Mom, tell her how horrible she is, what a bad mother she is, tell her in front of me, that way she can't lie," and somehow he would convince me to confront my mother, laying out the conditions he expected in exchange for his love.

After years of being the odd one out, Dad shined his light on me, smiled at me, wanted to talk to me. The desire to be loved by him was so strong that I ostracized Mom with zeal, with the kind of blind allegiance reserved for a cult leader. I began to do what he asked and tell Mom that she was horrible, and ask her why she didn't feed Jack, and she would cry, and get angry.

"What kind of mother do you think I am?" she would yell.

I didn't know, but Dad knew, and he said that she was the mother in this family, goddammit, and did she really think she could just do whatever she wanted?

When Mom and Dad sat us down and told us they were getting a divorce, Kyle and Jack started crying. I was relieved. Mom said we were moving and told us to pack a bag of essentials.

"For when we're in the car on the way to Port Alberni. It's on Vancouver Island, and there isn't a lot of space in the car. We'll have to send the rest by moving van."

I packed a toothbrush, my copy of *Richard III*, a pair of underwear, and a hairbrush into a yellow PUMA bag and didn't think about us leaving town. I decided to spend my remaining days with my friends, promising to write them letters and etching their faces in my memory.

Two days later, I was walking back from the mall with my friend Kim when Mom pulled up in a blue convertible with the top down. Another woman I had never seen before, a woman in her forties with cropped brown hair, full cheeks, and manicured nails, was leaning her arm across the steering wheel. She grinned at me. Kyle and Jack were in the backseat.

"Get in, hon," Mom called to me.

I was immediately suspicious.

"Why?"

"We're going to the beach."

"Oh, I'm good," I said. "I'll just hang with Kim and then go home and study for finals."

"I thought you'd want to do that, so I brought your schoolbooks along."

"Why would I want to study at the beach? That's the last place I would want to study."

Mom narrowed her eyes, and I narrowed mine. We stared at each other, neither one sure how to get the upper hand.

"Get in the car, Tanya."

Seeing I had no choice, I turned to Kim and gave her a hug. We stared at each other as I drove away, Kim standing with her feet on the pavement, and me flying in the opposite direction.

We were on the edge of town before Mom turned to us.

"Now, listen to me," she began, "your dad threatened to hurt us. It happened two days ago, and I didn't want to scare you, so I didn't say anything."

My forehead scrunched up, furrowed in confusion and disbelief.

"I talked to a lawyer, and he told me to look out for our safety. He said that your father could buy a gun or worse and I couldn't take any chances," Mom continued. "We have to leave for Port Alberni today, and we cannot under any circumstances call your father, or he will come and he will hurt us. You're going to have to trust me. You have to listen to everything that I say and do whatever I ask."

Mom's instructions hung in the air for a moment before they sunk in, a dead weight, into my consciousness. The word *gun* played on repeat in my head. *Gun, gun, gun.* Mom had used it to underline the gravity of the situation, to emphasize the extent of the danger. In my case, the word echoed in my brain until I thought she had told us that Dad had threatened to buy a gun and shoot us. I was forever haunted by the image of him hunting us like animals, but I questioned if he had threatened my mother or if she had been lying.

Kyle burst into tears and turned his face into the whipping wind, hiding in the crook of his arm. I watched the scene unfold around me. I sat back and stared at Mom, her black hair flying around her face in all directions. I was too overwhelmed to confront her and pulled my long arms inside my T-shirt to try to keep warm.

An hour passed before the car slowed. We were in a small town, smaller than Nelson. Quaint cottages and suburban houses lined the streets. Families were out playing with their kids, jumping through sprinklers and walking hand in hand down the sidewalk.

Pangs of rage welled up inside my body, the beginnings of an unquenchable anger. Dad had been paying so much attention to me, talking and caring for me in a way that he never had before. Just at the moment I was feeling accepted, like I was part of my father's world,

Mom had taken us from him and I hated her for it. And Dad had told us, over and over again, that she was a liar, that she would lie to us about him, about who he was, about what he did. So my first thought was that Mom was lying about Dad threatening us, and that everything she was doing was a ruse, an act blown out of the stratosphere, a daytime soap opera that only existed in Mom's head. We were a prisoner in her game with the added humiliation of going through it all with a complete stranger behind the wheel who knew more than us.

I wanted to talk to my brothers alone. Kyle was nine and could understand what was happening, but Jack was one and a half and had started crying because Kyle was in tears. He had no idea what was happening.

Mom pulled out an address from her oversized black leather purse. As she unfolded the paper, I glimpsed the address and realized we were in Trail, a small town about an hour from Nelson.

Mom and the woman looked around for street signs.

"Here we are," Mom chirped.

We pulled into a small cement driveway in front of a run-down tiny blue-and-white house. Mom got out and knocked on the front door, and the woman in the front seat turned to smile at us. I guessed that she was Mom's boss, since Mom's friends didn't drive sky-blue convertibles or get their nails done. I despised her but I didn't want her to leave. I wanted to drive back with her.

Mom turned to us and waved us over.

"Okay, remember to get your things," the woman in the car said to us.

Mom came to unlock Jack's car seat, then took it gently out of the convertible and put it down on the ground.

"Mom, I need a cigarette."

The woman from the car shot me a look.

"We can't risk you being out here by yourself, Tanya," Mom said. "You'll just have to wait."

"Nicky, I have to run back," Mom's boss said.

"Of course, Suzanne, thank you so much. I'll never forget you," Mom said.

Suzanne awkwardly hugged Mom, briskly got into her convertible, and sped away. I watched her, full of hatred, longing, and desperation. I never saw her again.

As I turned, there was a new stranger, a younger woman but rougher, with bags under her eyes, wavy shoulder-length hair, and a flowing flower-print dress. She extended her hand and motioned us toward the door.

"My name is Ellen, sweetheart," she said. "Don't worry about your shoes. Come inside, we have cookies."

What I wanted was a goddamned smoke. I followed my brothers and Mom into a small, sparse living room. There were posters on the wall of a tired woman holding a baby, a group of women standing in solidarity, and a field of flowers with the Lord's Prayer overlaid in curly type. I did not want a cookie here.

"Please, make yourself comfortable," Ellen said, motioning to a worn-out gray couch.

She disappeared for a second and returned with a tray of individually wrapped sugar cookies, white bread bologna sandwiches, a jug of milk, and pink plastic cups. I sat next to Kyle, passing him milk and a sandwich before I took one myself. I slowly put a piece of bread into my mouth and forced myself to swallow. Ellen smiled at us with the same patronizing expression that we got from Suzanne in the convertible. Mom crinkled and pulled at the plastic from one of the cookies and passed it to Jack, who devoured it and reached for another.

"So . . ." Ellen had somehow acquired a clipboard and pen. "Like I said before, I'm Ellen, and I work here at the Trail women's shelter. We talked on the phone a few days ago. You're staying for the afternoon?"

"Yes, we have a police officer coming to escort us to a truck in"— Mom looked at her watch—"four hours."

My head whipped in her direction as it became clear Mom had been carefully planning this move, plotting the how and the when every time Dad had taken us for dipped cones.

"You mentioned that on the phone. We have a few procedural questions we need to ask you, in case you need to come back here, or if the police need to find you. We won't give your information to anyone else, and you can rest assured this is a safe space and a discreet location."

Right, I thought, *the shittiest house on the block, with sad-looking mothers and their kids coming in and out. Yeah, no one knows what this place is.*

Ellen smiled and reached out to touch my mother, who exhaled deeply, what seemed to me a little too deeply, and then looked at me. Before we could lock eyes, I looked down at Ellen's hand touching Mom's arm and had the urge to rip Ellen's arm out of its socket. It was an empty touch, and to me it read like a choreographed gesture that she might have learned as a young counselor, meant to be executed when feigning understanding. Ellen clicked her pen and starting writing on her clipboard.

"Tell me your story, Nicky. How did you come to need our help?"

"Oh God, where do I start? My husband, my ex-husband, Marvin, he's an alcoholic, verbally and physically abusive. He yells at me, he takes our money and spends it all on himself, nothing on us. He controls every single part of our lives, where we go, who we see, when we eat. Sometimes he drinks the money away and there isn't enough for food. It's been so awful for me, just awful . . ."

Ellen was ticking boxes off on her paper. "Please continue."

"This is how it's been for years. Barely surviving, having to live under these horrendous conditions, and then finally, a month ago I got the courage and I told him that I was leaving."

Ellen looked up from her clipboard to give Mom an approving look.

"When I told Marvin I was moving out, he went off the deep end. He came home two days ago and told me that if we left, I would live to regret it. What could I do? I called a lawyer who told me to leave with the kids immediately, and that under no circumstances should I tell my ex-husband where I was going."

Mom's voice was shaky now. I wiped my hair away from my face, wishing we were anywhere else but where we were, that I was listening to anything else but this story. I wasn't shocked that Mom didn't send us out of the room before she talked to Ellen—neither parent censored us from the violence of their relationship, so hearing Mom talk about Dad like that wasn't strange. But the idea that Dad had been lying to us for the last few months and using us to upset Mom was too much to bear. I refused to believe it.

She continued.

"And that's when we found you. I called my mother and she told me to come to Port Alberni right away. I arranged for a police car to escort us to a truck. I work as an accountant at a trucking company, and I arranged for a driver to take us to my mother's. And I am so glad we found you, so glad. Oh, thank God we found you."

Mom slumped back in her chair, finishing her confession as Ellen turned to me.

"Tanya, that is your name, correct?"

"Yes, this is Tanya, the eldest. She's seen everything, she knows what's been going on, don't you, Tanya? Tell Ellen everything."

"I . . ."

"She's been treated so poorly, he put her below the other children, treats her like she's nothing."

"Well, I . . ."

"Go ahead, Tanya, tell her."

Ellen put her pen down. "We need to get information from your children. But I think it would be best if I speak to Tanya and your eldest son one-on-one."

"Why?" Mom asked.

"Procedure. We'll be right in the next room." Ellen stood up and opened a door off the living room.

Mom looked at me, pleading. I did not want to follow this woman anywhere.

"Just tell her what you know, Tanya. You know what's going on, you know the truth."

Behind the door was a small office. I took a seat in one of the fold-out chairs and Ellen sat behind her desk, her hands clasped over her papers. We stared at one another in silence for a long time. It seemed Ellen was waiting for me to open up.

"This is a confusing time for you, don't you think?" she finally said.

We fell into another silence, and I stared at my hands, folded into fists on my lap.

"Divorce can be a hard time for a family, yes?" she said, trying to pick up the conversation.

I didn't answer, so she tried a gentler approach.

"I'm here to help you, Tanya. Do you want to tell me what's going on?"

I wanted to tell Ellen that I didn't know what was going on. I wanted to tell her that Mom was full of shit, that Dad missed me and to please send me back home. I wanted to tell her that I was glad my parents were getting divorced, that Dad had hurt us, hurt us a lot but not enough to kill us, that he would never kill us. I wanted to tell Ellen that I was totally alone, that I wanted my friends, that I wanted to be understood.

"I don't know." I shrugged.

Ellen sighed.

"Have you been abused?"

"I guess."

"Has your father ever hit you? Ever threatened you?"

"I guess so."

Ellen leaned forward, looking directly at me.

"Is your mother telling the truth? Is that what it was like in your family?"

I took a long pause and looked at Ellen—gave her a full up and down with my eyes. Haggard, worn out, and probably overworked, Ellen didn't seem a threat at first, but she had taken me aside and she was challenging what my mom had said. Which meant she likely had the ability to separate us. On the one hand, she could send us back to Dad and to my friends, where I wanted to go. On the other, she could decide that neither parent was fit and put us all into foster care, possibly in separate homes, for who knows how long. Suddenly this sullen woman had the power, and though my loyalty within my family was skewed, my loyalty to my family, the only family I had, was unwavering.

"Yes," I said. "Yes, she's telling the truth."

A police officer came to pick us up later that afternoon. The first thing I noticed about him was that he had a gun—a pistol and a holster that clung to his thick leather belt. The presence of the gun was alarming, a siren that had sounded the moment the officer entered the room, and I tried to imagine Dad walking around with a weapon. The image was blurry, but for the first time it felt plausible, and further etched itself into my subconscious. The reality of being in a room with a loaded gun made me sit a little taller on the couch and ready myself for whatever we had to do next.

"Mrs. Marquardt?" The police officer shook Mom's hand.

"Remember to take all your things," Ellen said.

As we gathered our bags for the second time, I overheard Mom and Ellen talking.

"We'll never forget what you've done for us," Mom said.

Ellen shook our hands and watched us leave, holding the front door open for us as we followed the police officer to his cruiser. She watched us as we pulled away, our faces peeking over the top of the caged wire in the back window, her face receding in the distance.

We drove in silence. Two preteen kids and an infant sitting in the back of a cop cruiser, stuck in a car they couldn't escape, was absurd, even bordering on surreal. After I had talked with Ellen, she had pulled Kyle aside. I wanted to know what she'd asked him and what he'd told her. Kyle hadn't spoken to Mom, Jack, or me since that morning, which felt like a lifetime ago. Silence was how we were both protecting ourselves in that moment. But where my reaction was to remember every detail, creating a memory that became razor sharp, Kyle's was to forget, and I often wonder if these tactics started then, in the back of that car, the three of us side by side, tiny little criminals who had committed no crime.

Fifteen minutes passed before we turned off the highway into a grassy field. In the middle of the field was a parked semitruck. Mom got out of the car and headed to the truck while Jack, Kyle, and I stayed locked in the back with the bags in our laps until the cop let us out. We heaved our bags out of the car. I held Jack with one arm while I removed his car seat with the other, then walked over to the side of the semi to drop it next to the truck and pass Jack to Mom, who was talking with the cop and the truck driver. I turned and walked a few paces into the field.

"Don't go too far!" Mom yelled over the cop's shoulder at me.

I waved her away and stopped where I was, pulling my pack of Du Mauriers and a red lighter out of my pocket to light a smoke.

Sweet inhalation, smoke, flame, the heat filling my lungs, and I could feel my diaphragm pumping. Then exhalation and calm, the cloud of nicotine that I'd been wanting all day permeating my clothes and my breath, the taste of tobacco a pure pleasure in my mouth. A breeze teased the hair at the nape of my neck, rushing underneath my T-shirt and blowing my ponytail to and fro. The beginning of the evening surrounded me, cool wind coming to replace the midsummer heat.

The temporary nature of the day, and the explosive chaos of the past few hours were like heat crackling inside my head.

"Tanya, let's go," Mom snapped.

I rushed to the truck. "I'm hungry."

"In a bit. Go on, get in."

I clamored up the side of the truck and into the front seat. The truck driver was staring back at me. The first thing I noticed was that he didn't have a beer belly, and I thought that all truck drivers had beer bellies. He was medium build. Other than that he fit the stereotype I had in my mind, a cap pushed up on his head into a kind of cap bouffant, ripped-up pants, a checkered blue shirt, and cheap, unpolished work boots.

I surveyed the cab. A gigantic steering wheel was surrounded by buttons, levers, and speedometers, and when I glanced behind the seats into the back, which I found out later was called a *sleeper*, there was a bed where Jack and Kyle were sitting, staring blankly back at me. Jack looked tired and was fighting to keep his eyes open, the cowlick at the crown of his pudgy head sticking to his forehead.

"Thank you, thank you," Mom said, shaking the police officer's hand again. Then the cop got into his car and waited.

"He's not going to drive away until we do. We'll be safe." Mom started to get into the cab, passing me her purse as she clasped the edge of the truck door.

Did she think Dad was tracking us? Not wanting to contemplate the question, I stared at her, shocked by what she had implied.

"Tanya, move into the back." Mom was shoving me into the sleeper, so I passed into the back of the truck with Kyle and Jack where there was no window or ventilation. The air felt grimy, hanging and suspended in the grease and the dirt of the cab. The truck driver pulled onto the road and turned back to the highway, the field and the open air replaced by the timelessness of moving, of not knowing my surroundings.

Kyle lay down on his back and stared at the ceiling. Jack was dozing off beside him. With both of them beside each other on the bed, there wasn't room for me, so I sat in the front part of the sleeper, watching Mom and the truck driver. Mom wrapped her long arms around her torso and crossed her legs one on top of the other, tapping her foot anxiously.

"Oh thank God we're out of that mess," Mom said.

"Yep. Must have been a hard time," the truck driver agreed.

Mom interpreted the truck driver's "Yep" as an invitation to unload our private lives onto a complete stranger and launched into her monologue.

"It's been such a long, hard road to get here. My husband, my ex-husband, Marvin, he's an alcoholic, verbally and physically abusive. He yells at me, he takes our money and spends it all on himself, nothing on us. He controls every single part of our lives, where we go, who we see, when we eat. Sometimes he drinks . . ."

I listened to her repeat her story as she had told it to Ellen, her gestures and voice sounding as they had in that living room in Trail. There was an excitement underneath her explanations, her renderings of Dad and of our home life, a kind of exuberance, an enjoyment in her repetition of the facts, which were both accurate and exaggerated. I looked down at my hands, the sound of Mom's voice heavy and reverberating. The weight of what she was saying made me want to cry. But I couldn't. Any emotional outburst would have added to the drama, made me a willing participant in the narrative. The truck driver listened, nodding occasionally before checking his side mirror, a passive listener that Mom could pour her story into.

Eventually Mom stopped talking and stared out the passenger side window as the truck driver drove us westward. I reached into my bag and opened my copy of *Richard III*. Shakespeare's words were a comfort, and I flipped through the pages, looking at the way the words were laid out, neat verse after neat verse beating out a rhythm and a structure that

I could rely on, a map in the wilderness. It made me feel grounded. I didn't know where we were, or how long it would take to get to Port Alberni, but my mind latched onto the play like a comfort blanket and didn't let go until I had finished all five acts.

Hours passed and night fell without me noticing. When I looked up from the book, somewhere around Richard's death, my siblings were asleep. I was incredibly thirsty and there was a Vaseline-like film over every inch of my skin. My teeth felt fuzzy.

"Are we going to drive through the night?" I asked.

"Your Uncle Jim is going to meet us at the first ferry to Vancouver Island. I've timed it out, so yes, we do have to drive through the night. Just lay down, sweetheart. Try and get some sleep."

"There's no room back here. Is there anything to drink?"

"Got some water right here." The truck driver passed back a warm plastic water bottle.

"Thanks," I said, gulping back the stale hot water. Water poured down my throat, but gave me no relief.

Leaning my head forward into my chest, I crossed my arms and tried to sleep, but instead I passed the night in and out of a half sleep, the truck's bumps waking me long enough to take in a blur of sensation. The feeling of movement, the smell of the truck, Mom's head, her hair, the truck driver pulling on the clutch, the sound of Jack snoring, Kyle's unintelligible mumblings in his sleep, the stars and the streetlights coming into view through the front window. All this melded together, creating a chaos of minidreams, collaged and overlapped, asymmetrical and arrhythmic, matching the emotions that had been coursing through my body all day.

At some point I fell asleep for a longer period of time, because when I opened my eyes, morning light was pouring through the front window of the truck. I leaned forward and felt the pains of sleep, my shoulders and lower back straining as the world started to come into focus.

The first thing I saw were trees. Pines and evergreens. They were everywhere, inching their way up a steep hill. As my eyes followed the tree line, I saw that the steep incline was actually a mountain, and that we were surrounded by mountains, individual trees becoming a smear of green as my eyes moved to the horizon. A tiny beach sprawled out to my left, connecting to a dock with rows of boats around it. We were at a ferry terminal, parked in a lot filled with trucks, cars, and vans, lined up in front of a tollbooth. Mom was still and alert, her back straight, her eyes scanning all the people walking by.

"There he is, oh there he is." Mom opened the door and hopped out of the cab.

I watched Mom walk toward another stranger, this time a man in his midthirties with chin-length black hair, curly and alive like Mom's, but with violet eyes. He looked like a younger version of my grandfather, except he was wearing a leather jacket and blue jeans. A lit cigarette hung from his mouth.

That must be my Uncle Jim, I thought.

Mom came back to the truck.

"Kids, kids, come on, wake up. Get your stuff. Uncle Jim is here. He's going to take us to Port Alberni."

Kyle sat up groggily, dutifully grabbed his bag, and left the sleeper, sliding down the side of the cab. I passed Jack to Mom and gathered the rest of our stuff.

I braced myself against the driver's seat and jumped onto the pavement. The salty air entered my lungs, the morning starting to shake off the night before. Standing outside, I imagined us all from above, an aerial shot of two greasy-haired kids standing on the side of the road with three bags and a car seat, dirty, tired, shell-shocked children watching this new woman, this animated mother with a baby in her arms, striding up to yet another stranger, one that looked strangely familiar.

And for as long as I live I'll never forget what Mom said as she embraced
my Uncle Jim.

"I feel like I'm on *Oprah Winfrey*."

After the divorce, the four of us moved in with my grandmother and
her boyfriend, Stan, in Port Alberni, on Vancouver Island. We had never
known our grandmother. She had left my grandpa, mother, and Aunt
Eleanor in the middle of the night when Mom was three and my aunt
was a newborn. They didn't hear from her until Mom decided to find
her, when we were living in Nelson.

Beverley and Mom had developed a relationship quickly, making
up for years of abandonment by talking to each other on the phone for
hours, Mom secretive about what they talked about, like they were two
girlfriends making plans to sneak out of the house. Somewhere in those
secret midnight conversations, Mom forgave Beverly for leaving them,
forgave her for not reaching out sooner to ask for forgiveness. And when
Mom mentioned that she was leaving my dad, Beverley offered us a
place to stay until Mom found a job.

Unemployed, Beverley and Stan spent their days chain-smoking
Player's Light rolled with handmade filters. Stan was a crotchety old
man with a hunchback, a mismanaged beard, and an asthmatic dog
with matted hair.

One day Jack accidentally broke a plate, and Stan tried to lock him
in the hallway closet. I pushed past him, saying, "You can't do that,"
and let my brother out.

"That's the way we used to do it," he called to me.

Jack was crying for Mom and I held him while we sat in the back-
yard, waiting for her to come home. When she did, I told her about
what Stan had done, and although she never mentioned it or talked to
Stan about it in front of us, a few days later Mom got a job at the local

newspaper and moved us into a duplex, a set of low-income housing units across town. While we waited for our furniture, we walked around in the desolate house. When we were all together Dad moved us every year, which meant I could see myself living anywhere. I told everyone what the eldest daughter was supposed to tell everyone after a divorce, that life was better, that my parents would be happier. I made meals, I babysat Jack during work hours, I vacuumed stairs, I unpacked boxes.

The tension between Mom and Dad was palpable even though they lived in different towns, with Kyle, Jack, and I acting as go-betweens for two people who hated each other.

Mom, finding it more and more difficult to speak to Dad, would ask, "Could you just call your father and tell him . . ."

The thought of calling Dad to relay information from Mom made me nauseated, but so did the sound of them yelling at each other on the telephone. So I would call, and then Mom would force me to stay on the phone so she could listen in with the other receiver, whispering at me, telling me how to respond. Dad would say horrible things, Mom would have me retaliate for her, and after so many years of dysfunction, it felt like we had all come down with some horrible illness, except that we weren't allowed to admit that we were sick. After I would hang up the phone, exhausted from trying to appease both of my parents, I would go and hang out my window, smoking a cigarette while feeling the weight of my torso and the hard windowsill pressing into the flesh around my hips. It was a painful feeling but at least it was a feeling, the air cool and wet against my face, the pinching of my skin getting more intense with each inhalation.

The duplex was filled with kids, absentee parents, drug addicts, single mothers, and retired elderly ladies who would give you cigarettes if you kept them company on Sunday afternoons. I played football with a few of the boys who lived across the duplex from me, and had a crush on a kid named Phil, whose house smelled like Hamburger Helper. On my first day at the local junior high, a grunge boy sent me a love letter in rhyming couplets. I didn't know what to do, since the only romantic event in my life at that point had been an impromptu French kiss with a kid named Tony while slow-dancing to Zeppelin's "Stairway to Heaven." I spent the second day of classes holding hands with the grunge boy, and then sucking face with him in the woods near the baseball diamond. During the make-out session, the grunge boy's braces cut my lips. As I rolled my tongue inside his mouth, I felt all the way back to his tonsils.

It was near that duplex that I got drunk for the first time. Melanie, a girl I knew briefly in junior high, got her older brother to buy the liquor for my fourteenth birthday. Since I didn't know what kind of booze I'd like, I asked her to buy Dad's old standby, a bottle of Smirnoff and a two-litre of Coca-Cola.

The weekend I got drunk, Mom, Jack, and Kyle were visiting relatives. Melanie brought the booze over with her older brother and his friends, two older guys in jean jackets and baseball caps. We took the booze into the woods behind the duplex and walked down a rocky, narrow path until we got to the creek that ran through town. It was dusk in November, and I could barely see the bottle as I brought it to my lips. It tasted like hairspray, and I quickly slugged back some of the cola to wash the taste out of my mouth.

"Yuck," I said, spitting into the water.

Melanie's brother and his friends chuckled.

I passed the cola to Melanie, and she took a slug to wash down some of the whiskey she had bought for herself.

Drinking the liquor felt awful and then suddenly fortifying. Buzzing warmth spread from the place where the bottle kissed my mouth. My veins felt hot, like they were filling with electric blood, and the trees hummed along to the sound of the creek, a night song of wind and leaves and the rushing of water over rock. It was getting dark and I could barely see the outlines of Melanie and her brother. It seemed as if everything were vibrating and alive. I held my hand out, splaying my fingers, and closed one eye to see the water beyond. A passing sensation swept over me, the feeling that I was becoming the water, disappearing into the creek. It was very funny and I found myself laughing for no reason, the beginnings of a lifelong love affair with booze cemented where I sat on the grass.

Every year students were given a schedule book, a week-at-a-glance calendar meant to help keep track of assignments and school activities. Starting on my fourteenth birthday, I wrote "#1" in the upper left-hand corner of the space reserved for Fridays and Saturdays. On the inside of the back jacket, I kept a running tally. The numbers in the Friday and Saturday boxes kept track of how many drinks I'd had each weekend, and the tally on the back page was of how many times I had gotten drunk since my fourteenth birthday. I wanted a very high number, proof that I was hardcore and could out-drink anyone, including my friends, strangers, old rednecks, and high school seniors. Drinking booze became a marathon, and each vodka poured down my gullet felt like a lifesaving elixir, making me feel intensely, tricking me into thinking I was getting in touch with who I really was. I didn't know it was a lie because it felt good, and I never wanted that good feeling to stop. All I wanted was escape, and I didn't stop counting until I went to high school. The last number was somewhere near a hundred.

Kyle and Mom fought all the time. Kyle wanted to live with Dad, and Mom always said no when he asked. The more Mom said no, the more violent Kyle got.

One night Kyle refused to eat his dinner.

"You'll sit here until it's finished," Mom threatened.

"Fuck you!" Kyle screamed and kept screaming as he ran into the living room. His screams of "Fuck you" turned into rage, a howling animal sound.

Then Kyle took two bird figurines that Mom had bought on her last vacation with Dad, to Cancún. It was one of the only things Mom had brought that reminded her of Dad, and the first time she had ever gone on vacation to another country.

Kyle ran to the top of the stairs, yelling, inconsolable, unintelligible.

"Kyle, what are you doing? Don't you dare do anything to those!" Mom ran after him.

Then I saw the shattering, the red parrot wings and yellow beaks smashing against the wall at the bottom of the stairs. And that's when Mom broke down. Kyle slammed the door to his room shut, and Mom fell at the bottom of the stairs and drew her knees into her and wept. I watched her, not knowing what I could possibly say to make it better.

We only knew the language of violence. It was a harsh language, effective, exacting, like using a knife.

A few weeks after Kyle smashed the porcelain birds, I found him using my stereo without asking and instead of telling him to stop, I threw his tapes out the window.

"There. You can't use my stereo if you don't have anything to listen to," I said, chucking the last one into the deep woods behind our duplex.

Kyle ran into my room and before I could stop him, he set my purse on fire and left the ashen plastic remnants on my bedspread. I punched him in the arm, pulled him into the hallway, and threw him against the wall, not reacting at all to the hard thud of his eleven-year-old body as it hit.

We retreated to our rooms, attempting to annihilate each other through total silence, and spent days pretending that the other person didn't exist, walking to school without looking at each other. This scenario went on until Kyle retreated for longer periods of time, into the safety of his bedroom. We were mirroring what we had been taught, and it was the only way to release the trauma of what was happening to our family. We didn't have the words to express it, so we used our brute strength. When we did fight we also cried, punches acting like embraces as our fists landed, pummeling each other's bodies with love.

As a kid, Kyle couldn't remove himself from our life in Port Alberni, and so he began to withdraw. At first he stopped talking at the kitchen table, and then he stopped coming to the kitchen table, and after a while I stopped calling him down to dinner. Kyle stopped changing out of his pajamas on the weekends, and they soon became a uniform. His bedroom was permanently closed, and Kyle would use the bathroom or sneak food in the middle of the night, after Mom and I had gone to sleep. After a while he discovered computer games, each one an alternate universe, a parallel narrative where he was not a body in pain but a mind on a journey, and he stayed there for many years. Kyle became a ghost who wasn't really a ghost, like Bertha in *Jane Eyre* or Colin in *The Secret Garden*, and we judged him for it, called him lazy. I thought that his refusal to engage with Mom or with me was revenge for being taken away from Dad. I didn't realize it was self-preservation.

A year after we arrived on Vancouver Island, Mom met Don Flanagan. Our Aunt Luca thought they would make a cute couple and set them up on a blind date at a family reunion.

"I will probably be home in an hour," Mom scoffed before she left the house that night.

Mom had gotten a job as a receptionist at the local newspaper, and had a few offers for dates every week. She said no to all of them.

"Another jerk asked me to go for a drink today. The nerve to ask me out at work," Mom would say under her breath.

I would hear her tossing and turning in the middle of the night, could feel her loneliness on paydays when she would spend Friday night eating pizza with us and watching late-night romantic comedies instead of going to the bar with her girlfriends.

There was no reason to think the blind date would be any different. When she didn't come home until after midnight, her cheeks were flush and she went immediately to bed, hiding her excitement from me as she walked through the door and then left me downstairs with the TV on, where I was watching *When Harry Met Sally* on late night.

Don was an electrician twelve years her senior, with four kids, a camper van, and a rundown house. They hit it off right away. Mom quickly made us dinner every night so she could go upstairs and spend the remaining hours of the day on the phone talking to Don.

I reacted to the feeling that she was leaving us by rummaging through her blazers when she was at work, stealing the money I found to buy cigarettes and using the contours of my hands to search for the part of her that she was giving to this new stranger, squeezing her shoulder pads, pulling at the hem of her skirts hung neatly behind the jackets. Sometimes I would even lean into her clothes to be surrounded by her smell, a lilac that burned the inside of my nostrils.

Six months later, Mom informed Kyle, Jack, and me that we were moving into Don's place.

"I don't want to move in with him, I don't want to even be here!" Kyle yelled.

"Well, you don't have a choice," Mom replied.

"I don't want to move either," I echoed, backing Kyle for the first time in a long time.

"You'll see. You'll like it there." Mom picked up Jack and squeezed him to her chest. He was too young to say anything and hugged her back.

We met Don's kids one Friday night over two pizzas and a six-pack of Coke. Wayne, Theo, Evan, and Joanne.

"Tanya, you and Theo are in the same grade," Mom said, attempting to make small talk.

I nodded at Theo, but said nothing.

Kyle, Jack, and I sat on one side of the table and Don's kids sat on the other. We barely spoke the entire evening, just a few sideways glances and long silences punctuated by the gulping of soda.

As a table of kids from two broken homes, we all put on brave faces, stone-cold poker players sizing each other up and wondering which side was going to win. Years later we would become friends, aunts to children, and refer to each other as brothers and sisters. But at that moment Don's kids looked like children from another planet, and I had no idea how to deal with their version of fucked up, just as they had no idea what to expect from ours.

It didn't take long to sense the new family dynamic. Since we were moving into their house, we would be the ones to make concessions, and the choice was simple. Conform or concede. Because we couldn't control the rapid-fire decision our parents made to move in, we punished each other by becoming the worst versions of ourselves.

Wayne kept spare change in oversized Canadian Club whiskey bottles and thought all my friends were "faggots." Theo was a wrestler on the high school team. He ate, smoked pot, and kept to himself. Evan was twelve, the same age as Kyle, and taught Jack how to piss off Don's deck. He also had a knack for stealing my money and my smokes. Joanne was the only other girl in the house, and Mom thought it would be a good idea if Joanne and I shared a room. It wasn't. Two teenage girls who have sisterhood thrust upon them should never share a bedroom. After a few months Mom and Don gave us each a separate bedroom, and paired Evan and Jack together instead.

Mom was desperate to become a part of Don's family. She bought gifts for his kids and spent time with each one of them. When Evan would steal my money, Mom would say, "Well, you're the one who left it where he could find it."

We were the accessories to Mom's old life. Kyle, Jack, and I were left to fend for ourselves, ghosts in a house that we had never grown up in. It felt like she stopped seeing me, like I had disappeared. Jack was only three, and I could tell that he was confused about who these newfound strangers were. I felt the same. But Kyle saw the situation as his ticket to freedom.

At one of Don's family gatherings, Mom introduced Jack to Don's dad, saying, "Jack, this is your new grandpa."

Kyle grabbed Jack's hand and sat him on his lap. Jack looked awkward but open, looking around with a child's curiosity. Then, right in front of Mom's potential in-laws, he said, "Jack, that guy's not our grandfather. Don't be calling him shit like that."

He insulted Don on a daily basis, refused to talk to the new siblings, and kept up the fights with Mom.

Over dinner one night I heard Mom talking with my Auntie Luca. Luca kept saying that Kyle was "just like his father," a "bad egg" and an "unfortunate addition" to Mom's new family.

Two weeks later Kyle moved to Dad's.

These were the memories that went in and out of my mind as trees sped past the cab. I was shaking from nerves and the chill from the open window. The cabbie turned the corner and wound down a steep hill. We were driving into town and I sank down in my seat, hoping that Mom's car wouldn't pass me on her way home from work.

Arrival

Y ou can pull into that parking lot over there."

The cab pulled up next to a four-story apartment building that had an exterior covered in decaying stucco and mold and windows that looked waxy with grease. I could hear loud music coming from far off, too far to hear the words, but loud enough to make me wonder if I would sleep that night. The apartment was on a strip of about ten blocks that overlooked the Port Alberni pulp mill and reminded me of the opening credits of *Twin Peaks*, its two smoke stacks rising into nothingness. But instead of curvy women in black patent-leather shoes and detectives with a penchant for hot black coffee, there were mostly indigenous families, teenagers walking in and out of the Dairy Queen to chain-smoke cigarettes, and old ladies in pink polyester sweaters volunteering at thrift shops.

We were the only car in the parking lot. As the cab stopped, I slid forward on the cracked leather seat and saw my friend Liz standing near the far wall of the building, wiping her cropped bangs away from her face. Her boyfriend, Kristian, stood behind her, smoking and leaning against the building's whitewashed exterior.

"Thanks," I said, placing a twenty-dollar bill in the cabbie's hand. "Keep the change."

The cabbie didn't look at me as he released the trunk and I emptied the garbage bags from the back of the cab. Liz came over and put her hand on my shoulder, her brown eyes smiling at me.

"Hi, Tanya."

"Hey," I said, a sheepish grin spreading over my face as I slammed the trunk shut.

Liz and I had made a deal. Two months' stay, no longer. I would buy my own food and smokes, and, since Liz was five months pregnant, I wouldn't be a burden and would take care of myself.

"Is this all you brought?" Liz asked, surveying the plastic bags. "It's not much."

"Yeah, well . . ." I trailed off, not knowing what to say.

Moaning a little under his breath, Kristian heaved a garbage bag and a wine box into his arms while Liz picked up a bag of my socks. My lone backpack was all that was left on the pavement. I picked it up and followed my friends.

Kristian pried the building side door open with his foot, swinging it so hard that it slammed against the outside wall. He rushed inside before Liz and I hopped through the door, and a final gust of wind slammed the heavy steel shut behind me. The hallway smelled like mildew. I peered into the darkness and felt my body's resistance to walking up the stairs. Veins, muscles, blood, tendon, bones. All were screaming, *Turn around.*

"Tanya?" Liz called to me from the top of the stairs.

The sound of Liz's voice lulled me back into the present. I took a short gasp of air, as though I were about to dive headfirst into a pool of cold water, and stepped into the blackness, walking up the staircase one creaky step at a time.

As Kristian kicked open the door to their apartment, light flashed onto my face, the sun from a living room window painting the naked walls with its midevening glow.

"Drop everything in the living room," his voice floated back as I entered.

Liz told me I would be sleeping in the living room, so I threw my backpack next to an old Nintendo and scanned the apartment. There were no bookshelves, no plants, and no pictures in frames. There was only a bathroom, a kitchen, a bedroom, a living room, a couch, a couple of fold-out chairs, a coffee table, and a TV. I scratched my face, the insides of me feeling itchy as I continued to scan the space, doing what Dad had taught us do when he'd move us cross-country: assume that this new place was home and then look for evidence to support that claim, whether it was there or not.

This'll be all right, I lied to myself.

"I guess that's it." Liz pushed a grocery bag of my socks off the sofa and sat down.

"My mom can't do anything, you know," I said.

"You're sixteen now," Liz agreed. "The cops can't do anything either."

"She's such a fucking bitch," I said.

I was trying to be an adult, trying to encourage myself, but I didn't know what to do, so I sat next to Liz and leaned back until my skull touched the wall behind me. I was now living in an apartment with two other teenagers and no adults. The reality of that was so apparent that it stupefied us both. Liz's hand grazed her belly as she looked again at the pile I had brought into her home.

I waited until ten o'clock that night to call Mom. It barely rang before she answered the phone.

"Tell me where you are," Mom demanded.

"I'm not telling you that. I'm not coming home."

"What do you mean?" Mom's voice was high-pitched and trembling.

"I'm sixteen. You can't make me do anything. The cops won't help you."

I had been planning to say that for months, wanting to finally let out the venomous, seething rage I had been carrying around by taking control of my life. In the end, I said it in a voice that was barely above a whisper.

"That's bullshit. Where the hell are you!" she screamed.

"I'll call in a couple of days," I said. Then I hung up the phone.

Liz and Kristian's apartment building was host to a cast of characters. I never saw them during the day, but I heard them at night through paper-thin walls, raspy voices laughing over the blaring of a television, high-pitched sex screams or low gravelly swearing, crying children, the flicking sound of lighters, the clanging of bottles, and occasionally the cops, who could come in and out whenever they wanted, since the lock to the building was broken.

I slept on the blue-green couch in Liz and Kristian's living room. If I folded my blankets into a makeshift sleeping bag, the springs that stuck into my ribs wouldn't hurt as much, but it didn't matter. Sleep was rare. I was at the whim of Kristian, who barely slept and stayed up playing *Zelda* on the Nintendo until the sun came up.

Kristian was five feet tall with thick Coke-bottle glasses, a huge afro, and severe acne. He only wore black jeans and Ozzy Osbourne T-shirts and got disability checks from the government because of an emotional problem that he never specified, although he did tell me that he killed his friend's puppy by throwing it as hard as he could against the wall of his childhood bedroom.

"An accident," he said.

Despite his condition and the fact that he never went to high school, he had managed to meet and woo Liz at a house party. He'd shared his hard liquor with her before they had drunken sex in the storage room, the heavy metal music drowning out the sounds of their moans. After that they were inseparable.

A couple of months later Liz was pregnant. She decided to keep the baby and drop out of high school. Her father, an insurance salesman, set them up in an apartment and paid the rent and food bills that

Kristian couldn't pay with his small disability checks. Their plan was that Kristian would stay at home and take care of the baby while Liz went back to school.

Before Liz got pregnant she was a shy tomboy who wore plain T-shirts and cheap running shoes. After she got pregnant, Liz was sentimental and cried a lot about not knowing how to make chicken like her mom, and not being able to find the Windex or the matches to light the stove. I would listen to her and try to help her find the matches. Once I even went to a used bookstore to look for *The Joy of Cooking*. But I didn't know how to help her. As her pregnancy continued, she became more and more foreign to me, her body morphing and altering the landscape of the person I knew. Her pregnancy slowly cracked the fissure of our connection, and with each passing month the chasm between us widened until we behaved more like strangers than friends, smiling politely in the mornings when I passed her on my way to school.

Kristian liked to practice air-drumming to Ozzy Osbourne tapes. They had been played so much that the title of the album and the songs had rubbed off. I watched him, smoking along to his head-banging. After the Ozzy and hours of playing Nintendo, it would be well past midnight. We would turn the TV off and sit watching a single streetlamp glowing outside the window. Kristian would give me an Ozzy play-by-play, recounting all of Osbourne's musical influences and occult interests, starting with his transition to Black Sabbath front man and ending with the details of his lucrative solo career. Kristian would talk about wanting to be a famous drummer and I would encourage him. Then I would talk about wanting to be a famous actress.

"Do anything you can to get out of this place," Kristian would tell me.

One night, after a long silence, Kristian turned to me.

"I think I'm ready to be a father," he said. "I love her. I'm so fucking lucky to have them in my life."

There was fear in his voice, palpable underneath his words.

"I can't wait to see what kind of crazyass baby you and Liz have." I poked him and we both laughed. Then I corrected myself.

"The baby will be beautiful," I said.

We sat in the silence. At first there was only the pale fluorescent light of the streetlamp pouring onto our faces, like a fake moon with a black backdrop. Then the sky turned a pale blue and the lamppost shut off as the oranges and the reds of sunrise began. When the sun appeared, it was sudden, barely a sliver before exploding into a brilliant yellow circle.

Kristian took the sun as his cue to go to bed. He never liked clocks. I would wait for the clicking sound of his bedroom door shutting and try to pass out for a couple of hours, but it never worked. Just as I would start to fall asleep, I would have to wake up, a jolt that would pull me out of an exhaustive half sleep. Usually I had fallen asleep in my clothes, thinking it would provide me with a few more precious moments of rest. I would haul my body out of bed when my alarm went off, pull my backpack out from behind the couch, and careen through the apartment in an attempt to get out the door.

I had to get to school.

Classes were a blur for me, and I was a facade of a student. I never failed a class or missed an assignment, but I can't remember ever doing homework, and besides my English and theater classes, I was constantly falling asleep. In my biology class, the teacher would show us videos of insects and plant species. It was a battle to stay awake once he turned out the light, and I would feel sleep come on like a brick in the face. I would fight my body, wanting to shut down its need for sleep, for food, for liquid. There was no time for rest. I needed to stay awake. Unlike many of my friends, I loved classes, enjoyed discussions with my teachers. And somehow I knew, more than my friends did, that school was how I would get out of this place.

"Tanya's run away. She's got the Veresh stubbornness . . . I know, she doesn't understand what's out there for her . . . Yes, I told her that . . . yes . . . yes, I know. If she'd only listen to me . . ."

Mom was talking on the phone with my Aunt Luca, standing in front of me like I wasn't there. They had planned it—Aunt Luca called on cue a few minutes after I arrived. It had been a couple of weeks since I had left Don's house, and by then I had told Mom where I was. She had called one afternoon and offered to make me a meal so that we could talk.

"Don't try and take me back," I told her, "I'll just run away where you'll never find me."

She had looked into her options.

"Goddamn police won't do anything, social services won't do anything. They've passed this ridiculous law. Once a kid is sixteen they're 'independents.' As if a sixteen-year-old has any idea how to be independent. Well, I know, what are the cops for anyway? It's ridiculous, just ridiculous . . ."

By the end of the conversation, Mom was yelling into the phone. I leaned my head into my cupped hands and stared at her. Her hair fell in short, frizzy waves around her neck. My wavy blonde hair had grown so long that if I reached behind my back I could grab it without having to tip my head. Our eye colors matched, green with hazel flecks, but her cheekbones were less defined than mine. Our lean and slender arms were the same, our frames thin and frail. But Mom hid hers under flower-print button-up shirts and bright-yellow jackets with shoulder pads that were way too big for her. I hid mine with thrift-store finds from dollar bins, old-lady dresses, musty jackets, and yellowing T-shirts. We both looked like we were trying on our parents' clothes and failing miserably at playing house.

Watching her made me sad, but I didn't know why. How had our relationship come to this? We were unable to have a discussion face-to-face—there was a phone acting as a mediator. I wanted her to be some other mother, but I couldn't deny that she was my mother, and I couldn't deny her pain and that her talking on the phone was her way of showing me her pain. My head felt heavy in my hands, and I thought I might faint before her conversation was over.

When she got off the phone, she turned to me.

"That was your aunt. She thinks you're being an idiot. She thinks you should stay here for the night."

"No, thanks." I looked down at the table, fiddling with the place-mat so that I didn't have to look into Mom's eyes.

Mom made me a chicken sandwich and gave me a glass of milk. We sat at the table, Mom staring at me coldly, hoping her severe gaze would guilt me into staying. I swallowed the sandwich in three gulps, feeling the sting of her eyes, but said nothing.

"Please don't do this," Mom said between spurts of weeping. We were sitting in her car, in front of Liz and Kristian's apartment, after I had demanded she drive me back.

"Tanya, come home. What are you going to do by yourself? Who will take care of you?" She was crying so hard that I could barely make out her words. I turned away from her, toward the car window.

I wanted to be strong, to mask what I was feeling, but mostly I wanted to be nothing, like I had never been born, so that my mother would be crying for nothing and for no one. Instead, I was hiding my face so that I could fight the tears welling up in my eyes.

I held my pain like a tense fist, turning it over and over until it had transformed into a deep knot in my gut. There were a lot of people to be angry with, but Kyle was living with Dad, and Dad was far away, and Jack was an innocent bystander. The only person to direct my anger at was sitting next to me in that car.

"I can take care of myself," I said through gritted teeth.

I got out of the car, flung open the unlocked door to the apartment, and walked again into the darkness.

Any Shape You Want

Where there are sixteen-year-old girls who don't want to go home, there are forty-year-old men with shitty cars, Lucky Lager beer, and Export "A" cigarettes. I would find myself in the men's homes, with faucets that didn't work, moldy dishes piled next to the sink, smelly green carpet, and bright fluorescent light from the kitchen that I turned off as I arrived and sat down on the carpet, a sixteen-year-old girl watching TV in the dark with all her friends, who had been invited and who shimmered in the dim, flickering light from the television. Everyone shared the same ashtray and rolled cigarettes from the butts to savor the last of the tobacco.

My friend Abby and I would periodically go outside for some air. In a small town like Port Alberni, the night was crystal clear and dead quiet. We would go to a park across the street, swing on a swing set, and light each other's smokes with cheap matches, sitting close, telling each other secrets in hushed tones and holding hands because the cold air gave us goose bumps. When we got too cold we would stand up, adjust our cheap cotton miniskirts, and go back to the house of the forty-year-old man because we wanted another beer.

The forty-year-old man would pick out one of the sixteen-year-old girls, usually the one who looked the most out of place, the homely one with the cheap sneakers and the oversized sweater with the hole in the armpit. A few minutes later, he would be rubbing the back of her neck and invite her outside to share their own special cigarette and a Lucky Lager.

I saw all this—the way the forty-year-old man would pretend to listen to whatever friend had been chosen that evening, and when she shyly looked away, search out her eyes so that they could look directly at one another. I even got to the part with the special cigarette on the back porch myself once. He told me how pretty I was and how he wished I was just a bit older and how mature and smart I was. I had heard it all before, when I was twelve in my basement in Nelson with Dad's friend Jeff. So all his tricks were old hat, and they didn't go very far. I don't fully know why the man gave up on me, and I don't really care. I'm just thankful I didn't lose my virginity to a forty-year-old man in his dirty house with his dirty dishes. If I had to take a guess, I think what saved me was that I saw what he was doing, and he saw that I could see what he was doing. As long as I didn't get in his way, I could come along for the beer and the smokes, which was a large part of why I was there in the first place.

One of my girlfriends fell for the game. She took the cigarettes and later in the week, on her lunch hour from high school, the forty-year-old man brought her a six-inch pizza sub. My friend disappeared soon after, and the next time I saw her, she was pregnant.

I was waiting in the parking lot for Liz and Kristian to come home when Clint walked around the far corner of the apartment building, his black skater hoodie pulled over his head and dirty-blond hair jetting out wildly against his face.

"Hi. I saw you from my window. You're new to the apartment, aren't you?"

I shrugged.

"You alone? It's cold." His breath was hanging in the air around us.

"I'm waiting for my friends to come home. They have the keys. They'll be home any minute," I mumbled.

"Oh, you live here?" Clint stepped forward.

"I'm staying with friends for a bit. I'm on the second floor."

I could feel Clint taking me in with his eyes and felt heat coursing through my belly. I wasn't used to boys looking at me this way. It made me feel exposed, and I didn't like that, but also, I didn't want him to look away.

"I'm on the third floor, corner apartment." He paused for effect. "Do you know who I am?"

I did. Every girl I knew wanted to sleep with Clint. They thought he was sexy and powerful and could really "get you places." He went to Vancouver all the time. He was in his twenties and had his own apartment. He was smart. And he sold drugs.

I shrugged again.

Clint spoke sweetly and slowly. "Why don't you come upstairs and wait in my place? I'll make us a fried bologna sandwich."

I was hungry. When Clint opened the door to the apartment building, I didn't hesitate. I stepped inside.

"Who are you?" Clint half whispered as we walked up the stairs.

"Tanya." I swallowed my name, and he asked again.

When I said it again, Clint repeated it back to me, louder and more definitive.

"Tanya."

It was like he was naming me.

Clint opened the door to his apartment and I entered, noticing how short he was, his head almost grazing my shoulder as he walked into the living room.

"Come. Sit."

Clint pulled out a faded chair with a stuffed plastic seat and stainless-steel back. I sat down and put my elbows on an old card table. I watched Clint drop coagulated olive oil into an old frying pan, and the sizzle and the black smoke filled his apartment.

"I've seen you around before. Where are you from? Are you in school?" he called out through the haze.

"Yeah. I'm crashing with my friends Liz and Kristian."

"Right, I know them. I've hung out with Kristian."

"Cool."

My brain swirled with images of Clint and Kristian smoking joints to Ozzy Osbourne and leaning against the walls of Clint's apartment, the floor half-covered in crumpled paper and ripped paperbacks. I leaned over and saw *Romeo and Juliet* tossed against the far corner.

"You read Shakespeare?" I blurted out.

"Have done. You?"

"I love Shakespeare."

"Well, so do I." Clint put a fried bologna sandwich under my nose. Its pungent smell activated my guts. Something inside me wondered if I should eat the sandwich, not because it might be rotten, but because it might require something from me in return.

Clint sat next to me and dragged his chair closer.

"What do you love about him?" he asked.

Inside my chest there was a surge. I'd never had a conversation about Shakespeare before, not outside school.

"Shakespeare's words are so beautiful, and I, I don't know . . . the way he puts them together . . . it's so sad and beautiful at the same time, and I . . . I once read *Hamlet*, and I love his character and his . . ."

"Go on . . ." Clint's eyes were on me. I picked up the sandwich and took a nervous bite.

"His struggle and all the death and life, it feels real to me, and all the things Shakespeare says about all kinds of things, hate and death, grief, kings, falling, and . . ."

Clint listened to me talk about Shakespeare and then likened it to Leonard Cohen's poetry. As I rambled and ate, he walked over to a stack of CDs and started riffling through them.

"I want to play you something," he mumbled, interrupting my train of thought. "You ever heard of Einstürzende Neubauten?"

Clint turned to put the disc into his CD player.

I shook my head.

"German noise music is the shit." Clint passed me the CD jacket as the sound of a garbage can lid being dragged across cement started blaring through his speakers.

"Yeah. It's kind of off-putting," I said, genuinely enjoying the strange music.

Clint came back to the card table with a book. Its front jacket was faded, the pages folded and browning. He passed it to me.

"It's a copy of Cohen's *Beautiful Losers*. I read it in a high school English class before I dropped out. It's going to be a classic, don't you think?" And then he added, "You're smart. I'm lucky that Kristian wasn't home. I haven't talked like this in a long time."

I was silent and folded my arms across my chest, but I was looking at him, taking him in. I'd heard so much about Clint. Gossip mostly. That he did coke and sold it to high-schoolers like us. That he was on welfare. That he liked to sleep with virgins. That he gave some girl herpes and he had a son. And looking at his dirty face, his eyes on me, I suddenly had an aching desire to kiss him.

"I bet Kristian is home by now." I stood up and put on my gray hoodie. Clint watched me walk toward the door.

"Come back soon," he called after me, "I'd like to finish our conversation."

A couple of weeks later, Clint threw a party at his place, and I went with Liz and Kristian. They were the only people at the party that I knew. Everyone else was older and the music was loud when we walked in, so I went to an open window, slid down the wall, and lit a smoke. I scanned the room, looking for Clint.

He had called me a few times at Liz and Kristian's. We never had long conversations, but he always asked me how I was. I began having dreams of Clint kissing me in his bedroom, where he would take off my clothes and lay me down on his bed. In the dreams he would get on top of me and his skin would be warm. Then he would whisper over and over in my ear, *I love you, I love you, I love you.* At the end of the dream, the two of us would fall in love, and I would live with him for the rest of my life.

"Look what I found." Clint was standing over me. "You made it."

I smiled meekly back at him.

"Great." Clint sat down beside me. "You know what else I found?"

I shook my head.

"Here." Clint passed me a vodka and cola with a tilt of his head, an almost gentlemanly smile on his face. I was full of terror and longing. Clint stood up.

"Gotta make the rounds. Enjoy, okay?"

And Clint was off.

I drank a lot of vodka that night, and every time I thought about leaving, Clint would appear, delicately brushing his fingers across my shoulder, or I would see him from across the room, looking at me the same way he had a few weeks before, when I was cold and alone in the parking lot. But now I recognized the look. It was desire, and it made the evening swoon, filled with booze and talk, until I noticed that Liz and Kristian were gone.

It was late and I stood up to leave, but Clint walked over to me, took the cup from my hand, leaned over, and whispered, "Have I shown you my room?"

Clint steadied me by clasping his hand in mine, his palm grainy and fat against my long, slender fingers. The few stragglers left at the party looked at us as we moved toward Clint's room, knowing exactly where we were going and what was going to happen.

His bed was a flimsy mattress on the floor with brown translucent sheets thrown on top of a flat pillow with no case. Letting go of Clint's hand I went to sit on his bed and wrapped my arms around myself.

Clint closed the door and turned to face me. This time he avoided my eyes. Reaching back, he flicked off the light. I listened to the sound of his socks scuffing toward me and then felt him touch my shoulder, a delicate pressing to lay me flat on my back. He climbed onto the bed and embraced me, sweeping his hands under my shirt and pushing his forearms into my back. We lay there, me feeling him on top of me, the squeezing of his arms, the weight of his body on mine, the sinking into the folds of his mattress. It was suffocating.

This is it, I thought.

I wasn't sure what to do so I was still. Clint didn't try and take off my bra. He didn't touch my breasts or take off my shirt. He just held me in his uncomfortable way, both of us suspended and breathing in the darkness.

I wish I could say that Clint said something to me in that room, something to make me feel beautiful, something to make me feel calm. He said nothing. The side of his cheek was rough, and he buried it into my face. Both of us waited for a gesture, a movement, an open mouth, a reaching, a pushing away, or a turning over. There was nothing but the stillness of our bodies, the fear, and the anticipation. It seemed like forever, but after a couple of minutes in this awkward position, Clint sighed and released his arms from around my torso. He scuffled back across the room and flicked on the light. A bare bulb shone down into a windowless, airless room. I was still lying in the position Clint had put me in.

"Here." Clint offered his hand. "Let's go back to the party."

There were a couple of guys in the living room listening to music on low. They looked up as we entered and Clint dropped my hand and went over to them. Soon they were all talking. Clint never made eye contact with me. I stood in the living room waiting for them to invite me over, but they never did. After a few minutes I slipped out and went back downstairs to Liz and Kristian's. They had left the door unlocked, and I fell into a half sleep on the blue-green couch. Lying there, I imagined all the things that could have happened in Clint's room but didn't. I told myself that the next time I hung out with Clint, I would let him kiss me, I would open myself to him and let him do whatever he wanted.

The next day, I woke up with a raging hangover and called Clint's place, but there was no answer. I listened to the ringing, counting the space between each ring, but he never picked up. I figured he must have been hungover too and was sleeping it off. After three days of unanswered calls, it was clear. Because I hadn't slept with him, whatever had been between us was over.

Dust

"Okay, since this is your first session, we have to do a standard intake."

Mr. Phillips was the high school therapist. The school had arranged for him to come in when they found out I wasn't living at home, and though the sessions weren't mandatory, I went to avoid questions from the administration.

He fiddled with his papers, gathering them in a heap, making them neat, and then clipping them into a clipboard. His bouffant was falling into his eyes, and he was using his writing hand to brush the hair out of his face, his pencil sometimes acting as an accidental comb.

He doesn't know how to handle this, I thought to myself.

I glanced at the paper he was holding in his hand, and saw the myriad of numbered questions staring back at me in a bold font. I crossed my arms in front of my chest and leaned back in the chair, hungry and wanting nicotine.

"Again, they're standard questions and totally confidential."

I crossed my legs and nodded that he could start. The first round was rapid fire, with my answers overlapping his questions.

"How old are you?"

"Sixteen."

"Where do you live?"

"Port Alberni."

"What grade are you in?"

"Eleven."

I watched his gestures, the slow way he pushed the paper up after each series of questions, filling in the answers I provided. I imagined him erasing things after I left, writing notes in the margins, observations about how messed up I was and what he thought I wasn't telling him.

"What does your mother do?"

"She's a graphic designer at the local newspaper."

"And your father?"

"He's a door-to-door vacuum cleaner salesman."

Mr. Phillips looked up at me. Most adults paused when I told them what my father did for a living.

"Siblings?"

"Two. Kyle's three years younger than me, Jack is one, almost two."

"Is there substance abuse in your family?"

Oh great, we're going to talk about this, I thought and suddenly felt like a caged animal that Mr. Phillips was trying to lull toward him, so he could better observe me in my natural habitat.

"Yes. My father is an alcoholic."

"For how long?"

"As long as I can remember."

"Do you struggle with substance abuse?"

"Yes."

When he didn't ask any questions about the booze and the smokes, I was surprised. A sixteen-year-old with substance abuse issues seemed like a therapist's dream come true.

"Have you experienced physical abuse in your family?"

That too-familiar knot of nausea formed in my gut, despite my intentions to remain unmoved by Mr. Phillips's questions.

"Yes. My father."

"For how long?"

"As long as I can remember."

"Do you struggle with physical abuse?"

"No."

Mr. Phillips was simply checking "Yes" or "No" to the questions I answered. My life was his to-do list. I shifted in my seat, crossing my arms the opposite way and turned my legs away from him.

"Have you experienced verbal abuse in your family?"

"Yes."

"For how long?"

"For as long as I can remember."

"Do you struggle with verbal abuse?"

"No."

"Have you ever been suicidal?"

This was the first time an adult had asked me this question, and like the other questions on his clipboard, he asked me rapid fire. In spite of myself I brought my hands to my lips, looked out the window, and closed my eyes. The space between Mr. Phillips and me suddenly felt thick, and opening my eyes I saw that his face was tense. The longer I waited to answer, the more I got the impression that he didn't want me to answer it.

"Yes. I have been suicidal."

Mr. Phillips put down his pencil, visibly shaken.

"How old were you?"

For the first time in the interview I felt like he was genuinely asking a question.

"Eleven."

"Are you suicidal now?"

"No."

"Are you sure?"

"Yes."

"I am required by law to inform the authorities if you intend to hurt yourself or others."

"I know."

"So you're not suicidal?"

I was being asked a question, and at the same time Mr. Phillips was nodding at me, cueing me to answer in the negative. I had heard about what happened when teenagers tried to kill themselves. They were taken to quarantined rooms, sedated with drugs that had strange-sounding names, and tied down in their beds, and they couldn't go to the bathroom unless accompanied by old nurses with mean faces. They couldn't smoke cigarettes, and they couldn't see their friends until their parents signed a waiver. And so Mr. Phillips and I nodded at one another and made an unspoken agreement.

"No," I said, breaking the silence. "I'm not suicidal."

Mr. Phillips nodded, checking the "No" box.

"I'd like to see you once a week, Wednesdays, same time. I can help you. But for today, why don't we stop."

I swept my books and backpack into my arms and headed out the door.

Instead of going back to class after the session, I found a place to sit, beyond the football field, on the edge of a creek. I stopped myself from sobbing by lighting up a cigarette and looking into the rushing water.

My father's favorite punishment was to make my brother Kyle and me kneel in the corner, in the foyer of our house in Red Deer, Alberta. The foyer was cold and hard, with a floor made of gray marble, where Dad would loom over us.

"Pull up your pant legs."

If we didn't do it ourselves, he would force us, grabbing us by the shoulder and yanking our pant legs up against our will.

"No, Dad, no, please, we'll be good, please, no."

"Enough. In the corner. Now."

Once our knees were exposed he would make Kyle and me kneel side by side in the corner. At first I only felt cold stone against my flesh, but soon I would feel pressure against my kneecap and then the grainy texture of the hard stone tile digging into my knees, grinding into my skin until my kneecap was compressed. Then there would be pain, and if I stayed in the corner long enough, my legs would go numb, and if I stayed longer than that, I would feel nothing.

I would hear Kyle. He was seven and his breath was wavering and loud. I found it soothing to know that Kyle was there, but we were forbidden to make any sound. I would pray that Kyle wouldn't sniffle or cry out, but he was too young to control it.

"You little fucks, shut the fuck up, who do you think you are? Did I say you could move? Did I say you could fucking talk? I'll give you the fucking belt if you don't stop your goddamned sniveling. What are you, Kyle, a fucking baby? If you don't shut the fuck up, you'll be there all night."

Dad would sit behind us in a chair and Mom would disappear. I would strain my ears, longing for the sound of her footsteps and aching for the sound of her voice. I heard nothing.

Kyle got to go to bed first. He would fall asleep in the corner and Mom would reappear, sweeping in fast to gather Kyle into her arms and take him to his room, careful not to make a sound. I was left to kneel there, my face wet against the wall, my breath bouncing back against me, wondering why Mom had left me there, assuming that since I was the oldest my job was to take it, for her and for my brothers.

Once we were alone, Dad would drag his chair across the floor so that he was right behind me. He would crack beers or drink vodka, and when he got really drunk he would fall asleep in his chair. There would be stillness as his torso collapsed, his hand falling into his chest until it hit the seat and woke him up, heaving his uncontrollable limbs back to sitting.

All the while I would pray, *No more, please, no more, please, God, no more.*

Mom wouldn't come until Dad had passed out. There would be a hand on my shoulder and Mom's long fingers would clasp me with a firm grip as she slid me off the wall and led me toward my bedroom.

We never spoke to each other during those long walks down the hallway, never said anything to each other as she tucked me into bed. I never felt I had permission to speak, I didn't have the language to describe what I was feeling. PTSD, stress positions, psychological and emotional abuse—these are all words that other people have given me. The effects of what happened, the reality of how it broke my body, baffle me, almost like it happened to another person, not me. But I know that it happened to me. My body knows. It knows when I get on my knees to grab the Windex from under the island in the kitchen and the tile pushes up against that tender part of my knee, the tiny piece of skin on the left side of the kneecap that sends shooting pains through my nervous system. And it knows when I watch a father playing with his daughter in the park and I can't stop myself from wondering, *Is he hurting her?* even if every rational part of my being tells me otherwise, even if his eyes are wide and gentle like my grandfather's, whose love and care for me I've never questioned.

If I could have spoken to Mom as she tucked me into bed so long ago, I would have wept, and my mother would have wrapped her arms around me and listened to me weep. But we couldn't. I would climb into my bed and Mom would plug in my nightlight. After she left me, she would get Dad out of his chair and put him to bed. I would lay awake staring at the back of my door, the light from the streetlamp outside my window cascading through my bedroom. I was eleven.

At the school library, I read everything I could get my hands on. The librarian started me off with Judy Blume's *Are You There God? It's Me, Margaret,* but I thought it was too nice. Then she got me hooked on

The Baby-Sitters Club series and the Laura Ingalls Wilder books. I polished them off in less than two months and started looking for my own reading material, picking random books off the shelves. That's how I found *Hamlet*. I read and reread it, memorizing all his monologues and savoring the language. I found my favorite phrase: "The beauty of the world. The paragon of animals. And yet, to me, what is this quintessence of dust?"

That word, *quintessence*. I would say it to myself over and over again, lying faceup on my waterbed. *Quintessence. Quintessence.* I was afraid to look up the word. I worried that if I knew what quintessence meant, its mystery would be lost to me and there would be no pleasure in it.

Hamlet's girlfriend Ophelia drowned herself, "her garments, heavy with their drink . . . to muddy death." The moment I read that passage I knew. I wanted to die.

One day, before my parents came home from work, I filled the tub until it was almost overflowing and removed my clothes. I stepped into the porcelain tub and sank into the hot water. Folding my legs underneath me, I exhaled all the air from my lungs. Then I plunged my face into the water and slurped up the hot liquid in huge mouthfuls, inhaling and inhaling, trying to fill my lungs.

You can't die this way. Inevitably, I jerked up to sitting, sopping wet hair in my face, mucus and water pouring out of my nose and my mouth. I cried, tears mixing with the bathwater, but they weren't tears of sadness. They were tears of rage. I was angry at myself for being unable to do it, for not withstanding the sucking in of the water long enough to die. I leaned back in the tub until I was ready to try it again, and then again, and again, until I heard my parents come home, the door opening and the sound of grocery bags. By that point I was exhausted and had no energy left. Slipping into my pajamas, I went and lay on my waterbed, spread out like a starfish. The ceiling was wide and open, like the ocean.

In the Half-Light

Not long after Mom had moved us into Don's place, I met Garret at the convenience store near the Port Alberni high school on the lunch break between third and fourth period.

"I hear you can buy smokes," he said.

"Yeah, as long as you go in when there's no one around. I'm pretty tall so they barely card me."

"Fucking A. I'd go in myself but I look like an Aryan Bilbo Baggins, so . . ." Garret punched my arm lightly as he passed me a ten-dollar bill. He was short, shorter than most of the people I knew, but everyone was shorter than me. His hair was so blond it looked white, and it was longer than mine, and very shiny. I wasn't sure if I should buy cigarettes for him. There was a chance of getting carded, and once a cashier carded you, you wouldn't be able to buy cigarettes. After that, you would have to get someone else to buy them for you. It was a coveted position, and I couldn't read his eyes, which were blue, almost clear. I didn't know if he was worth the risk. Then Garret smiled at me like a kid about to trick the adults, raising one of his eyebrows. He mock pouted, his eyes still mischievous, which made him look like a demonic puppy. I laughed.

"Give it here," I said, snatching the bill.

Garret surrounded himself with a group of like-minded outcasts. There were goth kids clad in black with stainless-steel piercings in various parts of their bodies, dropouts, skater kids, hippies with nicotine-stained fingers, and Harold, the kid with diagnosed schizophrenia who only came to the convenience store at lunch hour and couldn't attend school because he had trouble integrating into conventional social

settings. And there were also closeted queers who, in the nineties in a
mill town like Port Alberni, were trying as hard as they could to stay in
the closet until college.

Garret was like me, a foul-mouthed chain-smoker, only he was a
foot shorter and male. I hovered above him like I did with all the boys,
who saw me as intimidating, mannish, and dark. Garret didn't seem
to care how I looked, what I said, or how I acted. He didn't mind my
unfeminine way of walking, like a half-broke horse, with a screeching
laugh and long, slender feet sloshing around in men's shoes.

My friend Stacy had suggested he ask me to buy him smokes. Stacy
had been one of my only friends when we first arrived in Port Alberni.
She had blood-red hair, emerald-green eyes, and looked like Glinda the
Good Witch from *The Wizard of Oz,* but slightly depressed and without
the glitzy crown. Stacy and Garret had been dating for a while and made
an odd match. Stacy was funny but soft-spoken, intelligent, and quiet.
Garret spent his time listening to death metal, playing the drums, and
yelling. But, somehow, it worked.

I became their third wheel when Stacy's parents refused to let them
see each other. Stacy would tell them that she was hanging out with me,
and then we would go spend time with Garret. This arrangement was
fine for me. I got smokes and great conversation, and Stacy and Garret
got to make out with me acting as lookout.

One afternoon Garret took us to an empty parking lot near the
Sears store.

"Who are we waiting for?" I asked.

"My friend Thomas," Garret said.

"Who's Thomas?"

"It doesn't matter. He doesn't go to school, okay? He's older."

Stacy and I glanced at each other. I felt weird about hanging around
with an older guy and wondered if we would end up drinking. I didn't
want to pretend to be sober in Stacy's parents' car and I didn't like

drinking if I couldn't get wasted. But Stacy shrugged in that "boys will be boys" kind of way, so I let it go.

A few minutes later, an older guy in his early twenties walked up. He had pockmarks on his face and a ball cap with a logo on it that I didn't recognize.

He swaggered over to Garret. "Hey."

"Hey, man." Garret took a step forward and then turned back to us. "Stay here," he ordered.

Now I was confused. Garret and Thomas did some posturing, a lot of handshakes and brash talk that I couldn't make out. Then Garret handed Thomas a twenty-dollar bill, turned back, and motioned us over.

"He buying pot?" I asked Stacy.

"I dunno. Probably," she sighed, walking over to Garret.

Garret introduced us to Thomas and we all nodded at each other.

"Okay, come with me," Thomas said, walking toward a side street.

"Where are we going?" I asked.

"Video store," Garret muttered, "shut it."

I turned to Stacy.

"What the fuck is going on?"

"Garret wants us to watch porn together," she explained, and before I could interject, she added, "We couldn't tell you, Tanya, because we knew you'd freak out. But you're the only person who could cover for me."

Stacy's eyes were begging, like a faun's, but they weren't winning me over. I had been duped and my face scrunched in disapproval.

"What?"

"Please, Tanya, Garret's been bothering me for a while. We're just going to watch the movie."

They were always doing this to me. Me, sitting in Garret's living room while they made out downstairs. Me, answering the phone and saying, "Oh, yes, Stacy's here, I'll get her to call you right back." And me, now expected to watch a pornographic film so that they could explore another facet of their sex life.

Stacy's parents were going to pick us up in the same parking lot where we had been hanging out, and we only had a couple of hours. If I left, her cover would be blown and she would be grounded for seeing Garret. I huffed and Stacy squeezed my hand. Then I turned from her and rolled my eyes.

There were only two video stores in town, the Blockbuster and a family-run store where you could find more obscure films. We were going to the family-run store, a tiny white building off a side road.

Thomas turned to us.

"What kind of video do you guys want?" he asked.

My nose wrinkled. *Gross.*

Stacy and Garret discussed in hushed voices until they had an answer for Thomas. I pretended that I was unaware and detached from the action.

We instinctively stopped at the bottom of the hill that led up to the video store and stood side by side. The hill was steep, and the store at the top was the reward. Stacy was quiet and stayed close to Garret. They were holding hands. Thomas took the first step, and I started to follow.

"No." Garret pulled at my shirt. "We can't all go in together, or they'll know Thomas is buying us the video."

"Right." I looked up at Thomas, who was shaking his hand at us without looking over his shoulder, a gesture telling us to stop and stay where we were.

"We can't wait here or the store might suspect," Garret said. "Stacy and I will go inside, then you. Just look at the videos, like you want to at something. After Thomas is done, we need to get the fuck outta there, but don't leave at the same time either. I'll go first, then Stacy, then Tanya. Make sure there's, like, ten seconds between the three of us. This way they won't suspect."

"Wouldn't it be better to just wait?" I asked. "Do they pay that much attention?"

Garret scoffed as he brushed past me and up the hill, taking Stacy by the hand.

This is so ridiculous, I thought to myself. *Our behavior is making us look more suspicious, not less.*

I waited the obligatory ten seconds and then walked up the hill. The door chimed as I stepped inside the store. It was a weekday at three p.m., and a couple of strangers were wandering the shelves, although they looked like they might be restocking so it was just the four of us.

Thomas headed toward a partitioned section of the store that had a sign on its door that read "PRIVATE: Minors Not Permitted."

Feeling sick to my stomach, I wondered where we were going to watch this video. I guessed Garret's place. We were about twenty minutes from his house, and we would barely have time to watch the video and come back to the parking lot.

I'll sit in another room once we get there, I thought, *maybe stay outside and smoke.*

It only took a couple of minutes before Thomas casually waltzed out of the private room with a videotape in his hands and went directly to the cashier. Stacy, Garret, and I couldn't help but look at each other, and realizing how suspicious we looked, we turned away and tried to avoid leaving the store at the exact same time.

The three of us were at the bottom of the hill before Thomas was finished renting the porno. He walked out of the store, a thick plastic bag swinging at his side, and took long strides toward us. As Thomas passed us, we followed close behind. Garret stepped forward quickly, effortlessly, and grabbed the plastic bag out of Thomas's hand. The exchange was complete.

"Come on," Garret called to Stacy and me.

Boys in front, girls in back, Garret and Thomas practically broke into a run. It was difficult to keep up. We were probably running because we had a ways to get to Garret's place.

When Garret led us up Thomas's driveway, I didn't say anything. I wasn't sure what to say, only that I felt implicated in what was happening and didn't feel like I could say no. I had been tricked, but I was so easy to trick. Stacy and Garret knew that my allegiance to their friendship was enough to secure my complacency. I was the poster girl for peer pressure and I tried to shrug it off, but the idea of walking into a strange man's house started a tremor in my body.

Thomas lived in a gigantic beige house with three cars in the driveway. He led us around the back, taking out his keys, and fiddled with the basement door before putting one of his keys in the lock and letting us inside.

There were a couple of steps into the basement and I tripped on one of them, stumbling in the dark after Garret and Stacy, feeling along the wall for support. I huffed as I found my footing. The basement was large, with a small window on the far side, where there was a living room, a couch, a couple of chairs, and a TV.

"Don't worry about your shoes," he said.

I had no idea who Thomas was, and from the moment I watched them shake hands earlier that afternoon, I could tell that Garret didn't know him well either. Garret had a knack for meeting the people in town who lived on the periphery, people who could get us access to drugs and alcohol and even a place to consume them. We would all pool our money together and Garret would appear forty-five minutes later with vodka, or a van would pull up and Garret would get inside and emerge later with a few bags of weed. He was connected. So connected he could arrange to have sex in a stranger's house while watching a porn movie.

"I can't believe we did it," Garret said triumphantly, "that it was that easy. Thomas, you're good."

"Uh-huh," Thomas replied.

Stacy was laughing at him, but she was nervously biting her lip and crossing and uncrossing her arms, her body folding in on itself. I didn't like the feeling in the room. It was as if Stacy were a sacrifice, the virginal offering at the end of some postmodern sex ritual. Or worse, the object that would complete Garret's teen-boy sex fantasy. Did Stacy agree to this? It wasn't that I couldn't imagine her watching or enjoying porn, but the setup was disturbing and reeked of male desperation.

I had seen porn before. Friends had shown me stashes of their dads' magazines, and once, during family movie night, we had flipped the channel and the screen flashed with the image of a woman sitting upright in a bed with large breasts flopping, a farmer with a straw hat and overalls sitting beside her.

"Oh, not this," Dad had said briskly, turning the channel quickly, all of us settling in to watch the kids' channel that he had ordered on pay-per-view, and me wondering, *What is going on?*

Garret took the video out of its case and passed it to Thomas. I lit up a smoke and passed the lighter to Garret, who lit up and then passed it to Thomas, three lit cigarettes in a cramped space. Thomas stood up and shoved the tape into the VHS machine and sat back onto the couch. Smoke billowed from our mouths, filling the room with white spirals and the strong smell of tobacco. The air was thick and our talking was replaced by heavy silence as the warning screen flickered on, something about having to be eighteen years of age or older to watch this video, and how violators would be prosecuted to the full extent of the law.

My spine straightened. It felt like my lungs were collapsing, my breath caught in my chest, and the smoking was acting like a respirator, the only thing keeping me from fainting. I can't remember anything about the video we watched. Every time I search my memory all I can manage is the warning screen and then it goes blurry. I know that I chain-smoked because I didn't want my hands to be empty, and that no one said anything. Usually Garret mocked everything we watched on television, but he didn't say a word about the porn movie, and neither did any of us.

About fifteen minutes into the movie, Garret and Stacy nodded at one another, stood up, and left through a door off the living room that I immediately registered as Thomas's bedroom. They shut the door behind them. I didn't want to be alone with Thomas listening to the fucking sounds coming from the television. Fear turned to nausea, which washed over me as I heard the turn of the lock. Every muscle in my body squeezed itself into a knot. I wanted to look stiff, like a dead body in rigor mortis.

With my body on high alert, I sat there faking that I was watching the porn. We didn't turn off the television, and I didn't know what Thomas was thinking, feeling, or watching. All I knew was that he never moved toward me, and that when he did move, to flick the ashes from his cigarette or light another, he didn't move quickly. He was quiet and deliberate, and both of us moved that way, staring straight ahead, not speaking, and moving only when absolutely necessary.

We sat for what seemed like forever, and Garret didn't open the door until the credits to the porn were rolling. He ran for the bathroom and Stacy appeared, leaning in the bedroom doorway. She was smiling, a huge grin that spread from ear to ear, a devilish smirk. Her cheeks were flush. They broke up a few months later.

Garret's mother was dying of lung cancer. I remember seeing her smoking in their living room, wrapped in a worn-out blanket on a sagging yellow couch. The house reeked of cigarettes and the curtains were drawn. Tubes came out of her nose, connecting her to a breathing machine. Her skeletal eyes were glued to the television.

"Let's go to the basement," Garret whispered. "I've got a couple of Export 'A' Greens down there."

Garret's father, Jacob, an older man with Garret's small frame and a full head of black hair, was putting a new VHS tape into the player for Garret's mom.

"Good night," he said, waving at us.

As we went downstairs, Garret looked over his shoulder.

"We record old reruns of *Star Trek* for her," he said. "We fucking love *Star Trek*."

Garret's mom died right before the summer break, a year before Garret graduated from high school. After the funeral he went to Vancouver and disappeared for the entire summer. I wanted to see him, and sometimes overheard that he had come into town for a night or two, but I never caught up with him and spent the summer before eleventh grade drinking vodka and blacking out on Southern Comfort.

On the first day back to school, I was walking to the store when I saw a familiar-looking boy standing in the alleyway. The boy was in a black velvet cloak pulled up over his head, with jet-black hair falling out onto his shoulders. It took me a minute to recognize who it was.

"Garret?"

Garret solemnly pulled back the cloak. His nose was pierced like a bull. Two studs poked out of his eyebrows, and he had two lip piercings on either side of his lower lip. All his clothes were black, and he was wearing twenty-holed steel-toe boots that made him taller than before.

"Garret?" I asked again.

At the time I didn't understand what a goth was, and Garret became the first one in our group. Like getting the last porcelain doll in a Royal Doulton collection, Garret completed the set. Our group now looked like something out of the Island of Misfit Toys. I was in total awe of him but I always had been, and Garret had spent the summer becoming well schooled in goth culture, from music to dress code to makeup, and was keen to be the teacher. Soon he was peddling mixed tapes of Ministry singles and introducing me to Siouxsie and the Banshees.

"They're similar to The Cure, but darker. And Siouxsie is fucking rad," he'd say, chucking me a mixed tape.

I was hesitant. I had been listening mostly to sixties music from living in Nelson, where I had embraced the local hippie culture and worn beaded necklaces and flowing wrap skirts with my running shoes. But that night I put the tape into my cassette deck and pressed play, and as soon as I heard Siouxsie's strong British accent, husky but also feminine under a dark, synthesized rhythm, melodious and inviting, I was hooked.

Garret played me Trent Reznor's music video "Broken," a series of cut-and-paste video clips of animal pornography and people shooting themselves. I didn't understand it, though Garret tried to explain it to me—something about American culture being overwhelmed by commodification and the resulting depression we feel at being controlled by the hidden politics of a truly fascist state. Or something like that. I wanted to know how Garret found out what a particular song meant, or about Danzig and "She Sells Sanctuary" by the Cult, or when Skinny Puppy was putting out their next album, or who Bauhaus was.

After his summer away, Garret starting having sex with anyone who would let him, and each act seemed like a kind of self-medication, a way to avoid dealing with his grief. Jacob let him have parties at the house, his mother's nicotine smell still lingering in the unwashed carpet, his death metal band, unnamed, playing in the corner of the basement at mind-searing volume. Garret would bang away at the drums and slam the cymbals, almost bashing his head with his own sticks, legs bouncing away at the pedals. Craig, the lead singer, screamed the lyrics like incantations. Kristian would air-drum while leaning against a wall like Garret's awkward twin, screaming along to Iron Maiden covers. I liked to lean against the fake wood paneling in Garret's basement and feel the reverberations of the drums against my spine. The music was way too loud, and we all drank way too much, and after the last set Garret would hone in on some girl, and I would end up passing out on the upstairs couch.

The morning after, he would tell me the details.

"You fucked her? I don't even remember Nadine being at the party."

"I told her she'd be a fucking fool if she didn't. Offered her some pot. Nadine loves pot, she can't say no. I got her to come over for an end-of-the-night joint."

"She has a boyfriend, Garret."

"That's not the point. The point is, I fucked her."

"How did you get her to do that?"

"It wasn't easy. I got her into my room but she wouldn't lay with me on the bed. Told me, 'I know what you want, I've heard all about you,' all that shit. Got her talking about the boyfriend, he seems like a douche."

"That worked?"

"What do you think?"

Garret took pride in getting the unobtainable girls, the popular ones with boyfriends who didn't want to be seen with him. Sometimes his conquests took weeks and I could never tell if he loved or hated them. As his curious friend, I was privy to the details of his conquests, and since I was "one of the boys," he said he would have sex with me only if I wanted to lose my virginity before I graduated high school. I think it was a genuine offer but at the time I felt repulsed by it, not because I thought he was being vastly overconfident but because he was my best friend and I wasn't attracted to him like that.

A few months before I ran away, Garret had a party, and I walked into his storage room to see my friend Michael kissing a skater guy. Michael didn't kiss guys. The skater guy was pressed against a table, and Michael was on top of him. Michael reached down, unzipped the skater guy's pants, and thrust his hand down there. He started giving the skater guy a hand job. They didn't notice me, or if they did, they didn't care. For me it was empty and vacuous, like watching *Saturday Night Live* while absentmindedly eating popcorn.

Live Through This

Abby lived two hours away, past the Tseshaht reservation, down a barely visible logging road, up a steep hill, and then down into the tall grass of a rundown trailer's lawn. I got to know Abby over the smokes we passed back and forth between us while sitting in her car, a white shitbox with a Barbie doll attached to the front bumper. Abby had taken black gaffer tape and wrapped it around the Barbie's legs and mouth, securing it to the car like a figurehead. She and the doll looked a lot alike, dressed in matching jean jackets and short, grungy skirts. Abby liked to extend black eyeliner off each of her lids with a flourish, and she took black marker and drew the same thick lines along the Barbie's eyelids. The doll's hair was left to whip wildly in the wind, just like Abby's, which was unkempt and knotted, often leaping around her face when she drove with the windows rolled down. I was barely able to find a clean pair of jeans to put on in the morning, and had zero fashion sense beyond T-shirts and used bell-bottoms from the thrift store. I found her enchanting, a strange creature, a punk creatrix that walked out of the forest and into our lives.

Abby loved to drive without any shoes on. I watched her stubby toes as I sat in the passenger seat, her black painted toenails fanning out to wrap around the brake or gas pedal. Abby's toes behaved like fingers, individual and dexterous. We'd park the car sometimes, push the front seats back, and lie together. Abby would wrap her toes around the mirror outside the car and play with it, pushing up and down, back and forth, side to side. I lay watching the mirror shift, reflecting images over and over again. A car, the school, guys walking down the street, the sky, the pavement. A car, the school, guys walking down the street, the sky, the pavement . . .

Because Abby's car was old and had no insulation, heat, or air-conditioning, it broke down constantly. We'd freeze in it during the winter and boil in it during the summer, but Abby was the only friend in our group who had a car, so we cherished it. When it did break down, which was often, Abby would step out of the car and pop the hood. She always knew how to fix the problem.

"Anyone got a rubber band or cup of water?" she would yell.

The first thing she did after we became friends was invite me to see what she'd stolen from the Biology Department.

"Hey, you wanna skip gym and sit in my car? I could show you my skulls," Abby said, kicking gravel into the road with her gritty work boots.

My eyes widened.

"Totally."

We drove a few blocks from the school, off a side road near a park, where Abby rolled us a couple of cigarettes. She balanced one smoke in her teeth while she rolled the other, pulled a red lighter out of her back pocket, and lit both cigarettes with one motion of her hand. Then she passed my smoke to me.

"Check it out," Abby said, nodding toward the glove box, squinting as the smoke from her cigarette got into her eyes.

I unhinged the creaking latch and slowly opened the glove box. Cradled against a mound of paper towel was a long glass container filled with translucent gray water.

"Go ahead." Abby exhaled, flicking her ash out the window. "It's dead, it's not gonna bite you."

I pulled the paper towel to the side, wrapped my hands around the glass container, and slid it carefully out of the glove box. I felt the weight of something moving around in the milky fluid, a pinkish thing that settled against the bottom of the container. Lifting it up toward my face, I tilted it into the sunlight and strained my eyes to see whatever was inside.

A mound of pink flesh the size of a clenched fist drifted toward the side of the jar, where I could make out two blue points and a snout. The eyes and teeth were gnarled, twisted like the fingers of an arthritic hand. It only had three legs. An umbilical cord, pink with blue veins all over it, floated in the viscous fluid along with the knuckle-like spinal column. Its belly and face looked like burnt white cheese.

"It's a deformed cat fetus," Abby said.

"What's it floating in?" I asked.

"Formaldehyde."

"Holy shit, dude. You stole this from Mr. Stevenson?"

"He hasn't said anything. I was checking it out for, like, months. Fucking coolest thing I've ever seen." Abby took the jar out of my hand and placed it in her lap.

Both of us examined the fetus in silent awe. My right hand slipped underneath my knee and I grabbed the warmth there. Abby stood the container upright and braced it between her bare thighs, the jar brushing against the hem of her cut-off jean shorts. I looked at her pointed nose, her greasy hair, and the cigarette dangling out of her mouth, her curved lips wrapped around the end. Her smoky brown eyes were wide, like her pupils wanted to crawl inside the jar. I had an overwhelming urge to kiss her.

"Coolest thing ever," Abby said, breaking the spell. I shook my head and sat upright.

"Think about it. This used to be inside a cat. A living cat." Abby slipped the jar back into the glove compartment and packed it in with paper towel. "I've got a couple of rat skulls in there too but they're superbreakable. Found them on my property. Leave 'em in there for now."

It seemed impossible to keep two skulls and a cat fetus in a glove compartment, but with Abby it didn't surprise me. She was nothing if not resourceful. I gently closed the creaking latch and Abby turned to me.

"Wan' another smoke?"

Licking the sticky part of her rolling paper with one hand, she turned on the ignition with the other and pumped the brake before we took off.

Parties at Abby's place were fun because her parents were never around.

"Hell, bring as many people as you want," she'd say. "My folks would rather have me party in the bush than in the city. At least then they know we can't get into too much trouble."

But you had to watch over Abby. The summer before I ran away, Abby had a party at her place. Garret got his dad to give us a ride, and we walked into the trailer with a forty pounder of vodka, Coca-Cola, a tent, and a couple of packs of smokes.

"Just add it to the bunch," Abby called from the living room, waving her hand toward the kitchen.

I set the vodka and Coke on the kitchen table next to a six-pack of Lucky Lager, three 26ers of gin, and a few two-litre jugs of peach-flavored Grower's "Canadian coolers."

Abby was sitting with Ryan, another friend in our group, a guitarist with an open smile and broad shoulders who always wore Cure T-shirts. Liz and Kristian were there, sinking into the cushions of a pullout and splitting a joint, the skunk smell wafting through the trailer.

I opened the cupboard, grabbed a plastic Slurpee cup, and mixed my first drink, vodka and lukewarm cola. The first drink was the best one. The *glug* sound of the vodka pouring into the huge plastic cup mixed with the fizzing cola sent waves of anticipation through my body.

Slayer's "Seasons in the Abyss" was in the CD player, loud and muffled from the crappy speakers in Abby's living room. Sitting on top of the speakers were stacks of books and *Heavy Metal* magazines. I grabbed a book and read the front jacket: *The Satanic Bible* by Anton LaVey. Wicked. I riffled through the pages while chugging the booze.

"This LaVey guy just sounds like a self-righteous asshole," I said, flinging the book on the floor next to a paperback copy of *The Hobbit.*

"No more than any of those Christian fuckers," Garret revved up. "Look at the fucking Crusades, man. Kill for Christ, it's the same bullshit the US government tells us about Iraq, the holier-than-thou, 'Let me fix your country, be like me, or I'm going to fucking blow you up' crap. Fucking Bush and Hitler would be in a circle jerk with Mussolini and Stalin if they all lived at the same time."

"Garret, don't you think you're going a bit overboard?" Ryan said. "I mean, sure, things are fucked up. I don't agree with the war either. But I doubt Bush and Hitler would be in a fucking circle jerk, man."

Garret leaned forward, red-faced, and yelled.

"The Gulf War is fucking systematic genocide, just like what the Nazis did. Shut down the theaters, shut down the radios, rules and regulations, segregation, population control through fear and propaganda, and finally submission and the willing relinquishing of freedom and control by the populace themselves."

Garret emphatically pounded his fist into his palm.

"Dude, enough, man! Enough. We get it." Ryan put a mixed tape into the tape deck. "It's fucking Friday. Let's listen to Danzig."

Danzig's baritone voice crooned "How the Gods Kill" and the death metal drowned out the political conversation. We bounced our heads up and down to the drums, getting swept away by the music. Halfway into my second drink, people's faces started to distort. By the time I had poured my third, the room was starting to spin. I felt immobilized and fell back into a plush green armchair.

Everyone else was just getting started. Someone had decided to blast the music and people were jumping up and down, head-banging in a frenzy. Liz, prepregnancy, had been quiet all night and stood up abruptly, swaying and pumping her fist. In no way was this swaying or pumping meant to be sexy. Liz was flailing around and tripping over the furniture. I could barely see her from my armchair. My eyes were half-open and I could smell the sugar from my drink and taste the syrupy sweetness in my mouth like stale puke.

Garret and Kristian stood up and unceremoniously removed Liz's shirt. I had seen them do this at other parties. Ryan was dancing beside them and head-banged over to the front door to exit so that he wouldn't have to witness the strange X-rated high school dance happening in Abby's living room. I could see his shadow by the potted plants, the smoke rising from his cigarette. Part of me wanted to be standing beside him, out in the warm air of the night, away from the blaring confusion and the violence of their touching, but I couldn't make my way to the door. I was too drunk.

Kristian yanked at the poorly upholstered pullout bed leaning against the far wall. A mattress with a pile of stained baby-blue sheets slammed to the ground. All three of them were laughing. Kristian and Garret took their shirts off. Liz wiggled out of her bra, her large nipples and massive breasts flopping in the half-light and the pot smoke. They looked shell-shocked, but they didn't stop. Liz licked her palm before slipping her hand into Kristian's pants, something I had seen her do a lot that summer. Kristian closed his eyes. I couldn't tell if he was in pain or if he was okay, and I wondered what he was feeling. I tried to answer these questions through my vodka haze while Liz and Kristian rolled out of their clothes and onto the pullout bed. I watched them and I couldn't stop. At some point Garret stopped being part of the action and sat next to the pullout bed in a small rocking chair, watching Liz and Kristian like I was. We glanced at one another and half smiled.

What they were doing should have fazed me. It should have shaken me in some way, if only from the oddity of seeing people perform intimate acts in a very public space. I felt instead like I was in the mud, an animal among animals, but on autopilot. My head spun and the room spiraled out of control until I blacked out.

When I came to, "Bela Lugosi's Dead" by Bauhaus was playing, its gothic bass vibrating the wall. It took everything in me to stay conscious. All I could do was try and hold onto the sensation of my feet inside my high-top sneakers, and the feeling of my sneakers against the shag carpet.

"Where's Abby?" Garret suddenly asked.

I barely heard Garret's question over the music but did hear the urgency in his voice and knew by his face what the urgency meant. We had to find Abby.

I stumbled toward the mass of limbs maneuvering on the pullout bed and shook the springs of the mattress.

"Dudes, come on, we gotta find Abby," I said. "Get your clothes on, we gotta find Abby."

I tumbled outside to get Ryan. Abby wasn't with him so we checked her car, where she usually went at the end of a party to listen to music and draw in her sketchbook. She wasn't there either. Ryan was about to go into the woods when I noticed that Abby's dog, Jacky, was missing.

"Where's Jacky?" I yelled at Ryan.

Ryan shook his head.

"Look for Jacky!" I called. "If we can find Jacky, we'll find Abby."

Ryan stayed outside in case Abby stumbled out of the forest, and I went back inside to check Abby's room. Kristian and Liz were passed out on the pullout bed. I started down the hallway for Abby's bedroom when I saw a light shimmering from under the bathroom door.

I knocked on the door. "Abby?"

"Get back."

"Abby?" I yelled over the music.

"Get the fuck back!" she cried, her voice cracking and high-pitched.

I started pounding with my fist.

"Abby, open the door. This isn't funny. Abby? Abby?"

The bathroom door was flimsy but locked, so I fiddled with the knob, jiggling it with one hand and pushing on the door with my shoulder. The door unlocked immediately.

I cracked the door slowly. Two large candles flickered on the back of the toilet, casting a soft but frenetic light, the mirror above the sink reflecting the deeper contents of the room. I peered into it, still afraid of what I might see. There was no shower curtain, the floor was littered with used towels, and then they were there, suddenly in focus, Jacky and Abby nestled together in the tub. Jacky was sitting upright, bewildered and damp. Abby was hitting herself repeatedly, her fists beating into her temples over and over again, and she was crying out like a rabid animal, a low, slow moaning.

"Fuck," I said.

Garret burst in, slamming the door open and flinching against the candlelight. His eyes widened as he took in the scene.

"I can't handle this, man, I'm on too much shit," he said, stumbling back into the living room.

My tongue felt numb, the only remnant of the drunk feeling I had felt the moment before. As the designated caretaker by default, I needed to be as sober as I could be and tried to assume a parental stance, the way my mother would stand above the tub with a towel when I was a little girl, waiting for me to jump out so she could dry me off. I was swaying and Abby was still keening in the half-light. I felt around on the counter, hiding my panic, the feeling of certainty in my bones. I had seen Abby like this at other parties and I knew how it ended.

We had all camped on her property earlier that summer, setting up tents while downing liquor and getting ready to party, a mass of dyed black hair against the bucolic backdrop. At first I didn't notice that Abby had disappeared. I was opening an apple cooler when she flung herself through the crowd, wailing as she fell to the grass with a thud.

There was so much blood coming out of her arm, the cuts sharp and surgical, running diagonally into her flesh. It was obvious the cuts had come from a razor blade, and they were so bad that we thought she had done serious damage and would need to go to the emergency room. No one wanted to go, but we had to get her father. By the time he arrived Abby had backed herself against a tree, holding her bloody arm and rocking back and forth. Abby's father sighed like he had seen it before.

"Get back, you guys," he said, pushing us away.

Abby cowered, whining like a wild dog as her father walked toward her.

"Abby, you're not an animal!" he yelled at her. "Pull yourself together. You're not an animal."

He kept yelling at her.

"Abby, you're not an animal. You're not an animal."

He yelled with a resigned determination until Abby was quiet. Once she stopped moaning he walked back to their trailer, leaving Abby to fend for herself. Abby stared straight ahead, squeezing her forearm with a strongman's grip. Knowing that we had to stop the blood, we dressed her wound with an old heavy metal T-shirt. I stood and stared, unsure of what I was watching, unsure how to help. *How did she get that razor blade? She was with us the whole time. Why did she transform into this wild animal? And where is she now, her cold eyes staring off into space?* I never got an answer. We were all too drunk to take her to the ER, and since her dad didn't seem to think the cuts were life-threatening, we decided that they weren't too. We let the moment pass and then kept partying, writing off Abby's cutting as something that "just happened" when she drank too much.

The razor blade had to be somewhere in the bathroom, and I hoped that Abby didn't still have it. Her parents were gone for the weekend and I didn't know how to drive, everyone was messed up, and we were two hours from the nearest hospital. Abby never told me why she cut herself and I never tried to talk to her about it. The silence was a kind of bond, one that we all made with one another, a pact to stick together, to be witnesses to each other's vast abnormalities without judgment, to accept each other's inconsistencies without demanding any change in behavior. We understood. Each of us was maneuvering, surviving. All we could do was stand next to each other, wait for the moment of escape. But in that bathroom, seeing all the blood running down her arm, I didn't care about Abby's reasons. I just wanted the razor blade.

I reached for her wrists and she flinched.

"Abby, let me see, Abby."

Abby didn't register anything I was saying to her. I got down on my hands and knees and tried to get eye to eye with her, the way a dog might, and made a soft cooing animal sound. Abby stopped yelping.

"You can't stop me. It's done, it's done." She started to cry.

"I know, just let me see, let me see," I said, slowing down my syllables, "I want to see, show me, Abby. Show me."

Abby turned to me and opened her palm. It was sweaty. At its center was the razor blade. I reached in slow motion so that I wouldn't frighten her. I kept cooing, keeping eye contact with her as I lifted the razor blade from her palm.

"Abby, I'm here. I'm here, Abby, look, look."

I reached for Abby's shoulder.

"No, no." She swatted at me and I saw blood coming out of a cut in her arm.

The wound ran lengthwise down Abby's forearm to just below the elbow. This was good. She hadn't tried to kill herself. She just wanted to cut. I needed to get her arm under the water and leaned back onto my haunches to turn on the cold water tap. Abby wasn't responding and didn't move when I tried to grab her arm. The soles of her feet were filthy. So were her arms. I needed to clean her wound before it got infected and I needed to get her attention.

My body knew what to do. I thrust my arm out toward her.

"Abby. Look."

Abby looked.

I took the razor blade and dug it into my left forearm, a small incision in the same place Abby had cut herself.

"See Abby? I love you. See? We're the same, Abby, we're the same."

The opening where my flesh met the razor blade was white, and as I cut I felt a tingling where I was slicing but no pain. The white beneath my skin parted and lipstick-red blood came pouring out. I held up my arm so Abby could see what I had done, and she snapped out of her haze and began to inspect my wound, wrapping her fingers around my outstretched wrist to look at the blood running down my arm and dripping off the tip of my elbow.

I took in short sipping breaths, careful not to wince as I breathed. The last thing I wanted to do was startle Abby after I had settled her, and I watched her watching me, watched her chest rise and fall, felt her heartbeat and the bloodied fingers of her hand. The room was thick and pungent, our sweat mixing together in the stale air all around us. With Abby's hand wrapped around my wrist, I could really see her cut. Placing my other hand on her shoulder and leaving Jacky curled in the tub, we stood up together and I pulled her toward the faucet, lowering her arm into the cold water. As it poured over her skin, I watched her eyes come back into focus. She let go of my arm to address her wound.

"There are some Band-Aids in the cabinet. Can you grab them?" she asked.

I handed them to her. Then I remembered my own wound. Blood was flowing down my arm, off my elbow and onto the floor, with dried blood crusting around the cut. The effects of the booze started to flood my body, making me light-headed. Abby and I looked at each other in the bathroom mirror and laughed.

After she cleaned her cut, Abby stumbled out of the bathroom and back to the party. Ryan came rushing in.

"Shit, Tanya, that's a deep cut," he said.

He ran my arm under the faucet and I watched in silence. The blood fell away like oil in water until the cut clotted and then we went back to the party.

I still have the scar.

What Remains

Mr. Walecki was pear-shaped. He liked to cross his arms on his belly, his shoes scuffing across the floor as he walked in a straight line back and forth in front of our English class, trying to convince sixteen-year-old Port Alberni boys, most who wanted to work at the local pulp mill, and the girls, who wanted to be the boys' future wives, that Shakespeare was relevant. I met him at the beginning of grade eleven, a couple of months before my sixteenth birthday. I lived for his class, and permanently marked up dog-eared pages of *Julius Caesar* with my BIC pen.

"Stuart, would you please read to us from the top of page 34, act 2, scene 2?" Mr. Walecki would say while Stuart's guy friends snickered.

"Go ahead, Stuart," Mr. Walecki would coax him in a dulcet tone.

"I don't see the point in learning all this," Stuart would mumble. Then he would take a breath and battle to speak out loud what he was reading on the page.

The boys hated being asked to read. They would hunch over, digging their fingers into the thick paper, and overarticulate words they didn't know how to pronounce. Listening to them struggle with the iambic pentameter was painful—a lot of "umms" and "What's this word?"—but I devoured it all, drawing my finger along each line of text the way a lover might draw a finger down a spine, feeling every vertebra in search of something deeper beneath the skin. I looked up words in the dictionary and dove into CliffsNotes. There was only so much I could understand, only so many experiences I could have. But I could feel the heartbeat of the pentameter in my blood.

"What are you writing there?"

Leaning my hip against a set of lockers, a used copy of *The Old Man and the Sea* cradled in my armpit, I was holding my diary open with my right hand and frantically writing in it with my left.

"Oh." I looked up, and the diary began to slide out of my hands.

Mr. Walecki was taking me in, inquisitive, his head tilted to one side as if he were looking at something peculiar. I clutched my diary to my chest to keep it from slamming to the ground.

"A poem. I was writing a poem."

"You're a writer then?" he asked.

No one had ever asked what I was writing, not friends, not family, and never an adult. At drunken bush parties I would bellow my poems out loud to crowds of onlookers, things to shock, the dirtier the better ("Masturbating in the dark of the night whispering *me / oh god fuck me fuck me fuck me harder / give me something to feel, to taste / push me harder, yeah, yeah, oh fuck yeah, more oh god.* silence / I slip into the kitchen / I make myself a sandwich"), but no one had ever named what I was doing, had ever called me a writer. It sent an electric buzz through my cheeks and I blushed.

"I guess so," I answered.

"Oh, how wonderful." Mr. Walecki peered into my diary like he was looking down a magic well. "Do you always draw pictures next to your poems?"

The diary was pressed against my body half-open, the unlined white pages covered in scribbles, poems and pen drawings of vines, eyeballs, and faceless women.

"Well"—I looked down to see my poems—"sometimes, I mean, if it feels right. I don't plan it or anything."

"Best way," Mr. Walecki said.

There was an uneasy silence and I began to gush, "I write a lot, I mean, I write all the time, poems and things mostly, they just come to me. They keep me up sometimes, I mean, you know, I can't seem to do anything without these words coming into my head, they're in there all the time. I write all the time. You know, I can't stop it really."

"I'd love to hear some," Mr. Walecki said.

I pulled the spiral binding of my diary to my sternum.

"Really?"

"Yes. How about Thursday, say, twenty minutes into lunch hour? Come to my room. Would that be okay?"

"Okay."

I asked myself, *Did I just say okay out loud?* and decided, *Yes, I did*—only it was a whisper, and I wondered if Mr. Walecki heard me.

"Okay," Mr. Walecki said, "Thursday it is."

When Thursday finally came, I smoked two cigarettes one after the other so that I would have five minutes to get to Mr. Walecki's classroom on time. The smoking was a tactic to try and slow my labored breathing. I had spent the week poring over my diary and had picked five poems I wanted to read. Most of them were untitled and none of them were upbeat. I loved them.

I stared up into Mr. Walecki's room. The sunlight hit his window at a sharp angle and reverberated off the glass. It blinded me. I let my cigarette dangle from my mouth, taking my usual hauls, the smoke billowing up into my face, and ash dropping off the tip onto the pebbled ground. I flipped through the torn pages of my diary, reading each poem under my breath. I was trying to find an order to the five I had selected, anxiously reading and rereading each stanza, my palms sweaty, my heart beating so fast that my fingers tingled.

I hope I don't faint, I thought, feeling a little light-headed.

After my second smoke, I launched myself up the steps. When I arrived at Mr. Walecki's room, I was out of breath and he was slowly unwrapping the wax from around a tuna fish sandwich. He also had a few cookies, a steel thermos of tea, and a kid's container of orange juice.

"Hello," he said.

I nodded quickly in his direction.

"You look flustered. Come in."

Feigning confidence, I strode into the room. I wasn't sure where to sit. I thought I should sit in the same desk that I did for class. I started to walk down the aisle but Mr. Walecki interrupted me.

"Oh, no, if you don't mind, I'd prefer you sit beside me. I'd like to see the way you lay out the poems on the page and embarrassingly, I'm a little hard of hearing." He shrugged to himself, accepting his age. "Would that be all right?" He motioned to the chair beside him, empty and waiting.

My eyes darted from the chair to his desk and back to him, and in that split second I assessed the distance between all three, deciding that it was safe.

The door to the room was wide open.

I took a deep breath, made horse-like strides over to the chair, and sat down.

I laid my diary in my lap. Clutching the top edge of the paper, my fingers wrapped around the cardboard cover, I waited for Mr. Walecki to say something. I was so excited that I felt like barfing and pissing my pants all at once. I wanted to read the poems aloud but had no idea how to start.

Mr. Walecki took a long bite of his tuna sandwich, slowly chewing with his brow furrowed.

"Did you know that when people first started to write poems, they memorized them?"

I shook my head, enraptured.

"Yes, they memorized the poems and later, when they wanted to share the poems, they would recite them out loud. Poems are meant to be heard, you see. That's why poets play with the way the poems are laid out on the page, the way they look. It says something to the reader about how to speak the words out loud. It says something about the rhythm of words."

Mr. Walecki hunched down in his chair and lowered his voice.

"I love that," he said, his eyes sparkling.

"I love that too," I blurted out.

I had no idea if what he was saying was accurate but I didn't care. All I could imagine were minstrels crying out in Old English from delicate parchment in town squares and knights yelling up through candlelit windows hoping that their love poems reached their lady loves to beckon them out onto their veranda, like in *Romeo and Juliet.*

"So then, let's have a listen. But before we do, have half my sandwich. My wife, dear heart, she always packs too much. I end up throwing half of it away."

Mr. Walecki moved the sandwich closer to me. I could see the mayo collecting on the wax paper and smelled the salt from the canned fish. My stomach convulsed in hunger. I looked up at him, desperate.

"Oh, go ahead. Really, you're doing me a favor. I hate throwing food away."

I reached for the sandwich and shoveled the first bite into my mouth. Celery, onion, fresh ground pepper, apple, and fish. It was intoxicating, and the protein instantly warmed my insides.

"Hmmm." I swallowed.

Mr. Walecki handed me a cup of tea.

"Now what do you have there?" He motioned to the diary balancing hands-free on my scrawny knees.

For the next six months, I visited Mr. Walecki. I read my poetry to him and he listened, leaning back in his chair with his arms folded on top of his belly, his head tilted to one side, and his bifocals clutched between the fingers of his left hand. His eyes would close like he was having a nap on a Sunday afternoon, perking up only to give instruction.

"Slow down, please," he would say or, "Could you read it once more?"

After I read the poem out loud, he would snap out of his half-waking state and sit up in his chair with a sharp inhale.

"Now why did you choose this word?" he would ask, or, "Why did you put a line break in the middle of this sentence?"

We would go over grammar, spelling, and layout while discussing possible edits. He never asked about the context for the writing and he showed no signs of alarm, shock, or disgust at the topics of suicide, hatred, loneliness, desperation, or despair. For this, I was grateful. After our poetry lunch breaks, I would go to the bathroom and cry, letting out big, wet teardrops that made echoing sounds as they tapped against the hard linoleum floor.

Afterward, I would often go to the school office, pick up the pencil sitting on the front desk, and sign myself out of classes for the rest of the day.

The mousy secretary whined the first time I did it, her head barely peeking over the front counter.

"We need your mother's permission," she said.

Looking down into her gray eyes, hard, stern, and disapproving, I flung my backpack over my shoulder.

"No, you don't," I told her. "I don't live at home. I give myself permission."

Signing with a flourish, I exited loudly through the front doors.

The Space Between

"You can't stay here anymore."

Liz's words didn't surprise me. I had stayed almost a month longer than I said I would, and she was right to ask me to leave. The Liz I had known, a scared-shitless kid from Alberta who drank too much beer and got into trouble, didn't exist anymore. She was looking at me the way my mother did, scolding and pleading with me to be semiadult about the fact that she was kicking me out.

"It's not you, Tanya, it's that I have to make room for my family. Kristian's going to be a father. We have to be a family now. You understand, right?"

I saw that Liz's cheeks were rosy and full of heat. She was hiding from the sun by standing in the doorway between the kitchen and the living room, a hand resting on her middle, her full belly protruding from under her gray sweatshirt.

We were all sitting in Liz and Kristian's apartment, Liz waiting for me to say something. I nodded in agreement and swiveled my lighter in circles on the coffee table, spinning it like a wheel. Kristian was sitting in his air-drumming chair, playing with his fingers and staring at the floor.

Later, they went to dinner with Liz's dad, and I waved to them from the living room window before crossing my arms around my chest. My fingers slipped into the cavities between my ribs, stretching over hard bone to squeeze my ribcage. I leaned my pelvis against the windowsill, my eyes focused on the landscape and the steely gray lamppost in the alley behind their apartment.

What are you feeling? I asked myself.

Leaning my head against the window, I looked at the flecks of black in the gray carpet and heard the fridge in the kitchen turn off. The green couch was still in the corner of the room and my stuff was still beside it. I lit a cigarette and closed my eyes, searching inside for any feeling about what had just happened to me. My lungs filled with velveteen gray smoke and the windowpane let off a cool wetness. Taking one last drag, I walked over to the couch and stubbed my cigarette out in the ashtray.

I had no idea what I was going to do. I could see that. I could see everything. The problem was that I felt nothing.

"Heard you need a place to stay."

I was wrapped in my winter jacket, the brittle rubber soles of my shoes rubbing against the gravel parking lot beside the convenience store. Stacy stepped toward me, her auburn hair sharp as roses against the snowy ground.

"I can't go home," I said.

"You can stay with me."

Stacy had overheard that I was looking for a place to stay and found me hanging out at my usual spot outside the store. Her offer was direct, but her voice was gentle.

"Really?"

I hadn't expected Stacy to help. We had fallen out of touch after she and Garret split up, and Stacy started spending time with a new bookish crowd.

"Yeah, I talked to my parents," Stacy said. "We figured it all out. My dad and I will come get you on Sunday. You're at that place on Argyle, right? With Liz and Kristian?"

"Wow. Yes, thank you."

Stacy shrugged, a "no big deal" gesture, and smiled.

"Well, see ya later," she said. "I gotta get to class."

I was at a loss for words and kept my eyes on her as she walked away, watching her until she became a small red dot disappearing into the crowd.

After Liz and Kristian had asked me to leave, I'd asked everyone I knew if I could stay with them. Garret's place was a no—there was no room and his father was still grieving the loss of his wife. Abby was a kind-of—her parents said I could spend the occasional weekend there if I needed to, but were noncommittal. I went back to Garret to see if I could stay for a couple of weekends a month and started to plan a piecemeal sleep schedule—a night here, two nights there. I was trying to stay focused on the task, furiously committed to staying away from Mom. But as the deadline loomed, I stopped sleeping altogether, lying on the couch, thinking that maybe the painful springs weren't that painful and wondering where I would be sleeping next.

Stacy's offer was so unexpected that it didn't seem real, eliminating the problem of my housing with such ease that I almost couldn't believe it was happening.

That weekend, her father came to pick me up. It was snowing and icy. My bones felt cold from the inside. I was wearing a drafty winter jacket with an inside lining that smelled like moldy cologne. It had been on sale at the local consignment shop, and I had bought it on the last Friday of the month, when you could get a garbage bag of clothes for five bucks.

Liz and Kristian were making dinner in the kitchen. We were all downplaying the obvious, acting like it was another typical day in the apartment. I kept feeling that I should say something to lighten the mood, but nothing was coming to mind. The chaos of my life had started to wear on me, the afternoons spent wandering grocery store parking lots asking strangers for cigarettes and nights spent sitting in parks doing my homework with my gloves on to give Liz and Kristian space.

The silence was our way of saying goodbye. It didn't seem fair that I had to go. I was enjoying my freedom, even if it did make me hungry, cold, and desperate. But it was late January, and it was getting harder to survive. I didn't have a job, and Dad only wired me thirty-five dollars a week.

"Might as well give the child support to you. Your mother just spends it on her fancy clothes," Dad said.

I didn't agree with him but I didn't correct him either. After we had settled in Port Alberni and Kyle moved in with him, I grew tired of Mom and Dad's fighting. If I had to listen to Dad complain for a half hour a week, I didn't care. I needed the money.

I used the money to buy peanut butter, white bread, a gallon of milk, cheap ramen noodles, and a pack of cigarettes. The cigarettes would run out first, followed by the ramen, the peanut butter, the white bread, and the milk. By Wednesday, I was bumming smokes and eating a single meal a day. By Friday, there would be nothing, but there would usually be a party, and friends would take pity on me and give me a shot of vodka, or a cheap cooler, and I would raid their fridge that night and the following morning. Saturday night would be much of the same, but by the following Sunday I was so hungry that I would go to the bank every hour, desperate to eat and buy a pack of cigarettes.

I can't fathom what living like this did to my body, my protruding ribs hiding underneath men's hoodies and flared bell-bottoms. I can't fathom what I carry still. Every time a meal is put in front of me, there is the feeling that it might be my last full meal, and like a feral cat I will eat whatever is on my plate in three gulps, a race to the finish line. It is only fairly recently that I've stopped having digestive problems. My insides were always hurting, aching like a punch in slow motion. The thing is, after a while I didn't notice the hunger, and as a runaway, I chose to satiate the unending hunger with nicotine and bought packs of smokes instead of bags of apples. There was no one to tell me not to, no hall monitor, no mother. I told myself that it was freeing to live this way, and in a way, it was. I answered to no one. But every Sunday, when I looked down at the meager amount of food that I had scrounged together and laid it on the living room table, I had to talk myself out of a panic attack.

When we were desperate, Kristian and I would collect cigarette butts. As a man without scruples, Kristian had no problem picking butts off the sidewalk—crushed butts, half-smoked menthols, day-old Export "A"s with fuchsia lipstick on the tip. I would hold the collected booty in the palm of my hand until we could go to the apartment and extract the tobacco from the butts, Kristian twisting the rolling paper until the tobacco would burst out onto the coffee table.

When we couldn't find butts on the street, we went to the local hospital and crept around the outdoor ashtrays.

"This place is a gold mine. I've found practically whole cigarettes in the ashtrays here," Kristian said as we walked into the ER parking lot of the old hospital. "People don't have time to smoke a whole smoke."

"Why not?" I asked.

"I dunno," Kristian replied, and then jokingly added, "Too old? Falling into a coma?"

"We should just quit. This is crazy," I said.

"What's the point? We're all firing nails into our coffins no matter what we do. Some of us are just nailing the pegs in a little faster, that's all." Kristian nodded in triumph, waving a half-smoked menthol.

Well, that's Kristian logic, I said to myself. *That's Kristian logic.*

Stacy scared us when she knocked on the door. Kristian and I made eye contact as I put on my jacket, attempting to make myself look present-able while Liz went to let Stacy in.

Stacy's dad entered first, his eyes darting around the room. He was small, a little over five feet tall and short like Stacy, but stout. In his checkered blue work shirt and brown leather workman's boots, he looked like he could throw a punch if he needed to.

"Tanya, this is my dad, Frank O'Connor."

Frank held out his hand. "Good to meetcha," he said, his voice bright and tinny.

I nodded back in his direction and we clasped hands. He squeezed my palm and I could feel the strength of his grip. It hurt slightly, but I was used to the workman's grip and tried to match it with my long and slender fingers, each of us taking in the other with a steady gaze.

"So then," he said, "where are your things?"

"They're over there." Liz pointed to the television, where I had once again piled my things in the corner by the Nintendo, filling garbage bags and cardboard boxes with my books, blankets, pillows, bathroom stuff, and clothes. I smiled at Frank, a meek, shameful smile, one that attempted to cover up my vulnerability. But it didn't. I was a child who had been living on a couch. I had accumulated nothing. The bags looked exactly the same as when I had moved in.

"Okay then." Frank lifted half the boxes in one sweep.

"Let me help you."

"I got it." Frank smiled. "You grab some more boxes. Let's get this all out in one go."

I got the impression that Frank wanted to spend as little time in the apartment as possible. It had been my home, and he zipped in and out of it in lightning speed, careful not to touch anything on the way out.

Kristian and I grabbed the bags and boxes and Stacy took the duvet and pillows. Frank's large silver pickup truck was idling in the parking lot with the side door open.

"If you girls don't mind sitting in the front together, I think we can fit all Tanya's things behind the seats. A couple of the bags might have to sit in the back of the truck, but it'll have to do."

"Thanks, Mr. O'Connor," I said, smiling at Stacy as she climbed into the truck to sit in the center.

"Call me Frank. Go on up and say goodbye if you like," he said. "We'll wait for you."

Kristian and I ran back into the building. There was no trace of me in the apartment. I scanned the couch and the coffee table. Liz and Kristian watched me, looking pensive, almost impatient.

"Well, I got everything," I assured them.

Liz walked me out into the hallway and gave me a half hug, one shoulder touching mine, and patted me lightly on the back.

"Come and see us whenever you want," she said, opening the door to her apartment.

"I will. Thanks again, you guys."

Liz nodded and turned to face me. Kristian stood behind her, leaning against the wall that separated the kitchen from the living room. They stood in the same way they had on my birthday, when I first arrived at their place. But now they looked different, more grown-up. Liz had an apron on. Kristian's face looked serious. They looked like a family.

I have no memory of seeing them after that.

Stacy's house was warm, and as I stepped in the front door, the warmth was all around me, like an embrace that smelled of houseplants and roasting meat. I had forgotten that feeling and was instantly enraptured by it, standing in front of the open door with my mouth half-open, as if I were witnessing a miracle.

Stacy's mom waved at me from the kitchen. She was blonde, slim, and put-together, with a not-too-tight pair of slacks on, a flower-print button-down shirt, and a teal-green V-neck sweater. She looked like a young Martha Stewart, comfortable, understated, and feminine. She was the exact opposite of my mom, and I didn't know what to say to her.

"Come on." Stacy heaved a bag of my clothes into her arms and marched up the stairs. I followed.

"My bedroom's at the top. Bathroom is next to me, and my parents' room is down the hall," she mumbled, reaching the top step and opening her bedroom door with her hip.

They had set up a bed for me on the floor in Stacy's room, a mattress covered in down blankets, sheets, and pillows.

"Oh, wow, Stace, that's amazing."

The idea that I was going to get a whole night's sleep in an actual bed made me want to cry, and I had to fight back the tears by pressing my face into the green garbage bags in my arms.

"What's amazing?" she said, putting my stuff down by her dresser.

"Everything," I gasped, "everything."

After I put my things away, Stacy's mom called me downstairs. Stacy was lounging on her bed, reading a book.

"I'll stay up here," she said.

When I came downstairs, Stacy's mom was sitting at the kitchen table with a pad of paper in front of her. She smiled warmly and motioned me to sit, but I knew we weren't going to gab over a cup of tea. Now was the time for "the talk," similar to the one Liz and I had had a few months prior. The pad of paper was the contract, a rental agreement of sorts, and though it was blank, I was certain that the terms were nonnegotiable.

"Stacy let us know about your situation, and we are prepared to help you but we cannot support you." She began writing on the legal pad, a planned gesture to emphasize whatever she was writing.

"I understand," I said.

Stacy's mom passed the pad of paper to me. It was an itemized budget.

"You have a month to find a job. I've calculated the cost of your food and utilities and you'll need to pay $300 a month. Can you agree to that?"

"Yes, of course," I said. I would have agreed to anything.

"If after a month you can't find something, you'll have to find another place to stay. I'm sorry, but it's the only way this is going to work."

Stacy's mom put her hand on mine and it felt motherly. I didn't like its patronizing quality and it reminded me of the empty gestures of other surrogate parental figures over the years, but I didn't want to disappoint her so I nodded emphatically.

"Thank you, Mrs. O'Connor," I replied in the most polite voice I could.

"You're welcome." She left the pad in front of me. I didn't reach to take it. "Did you get settled in okay?"

"Yes, thank you." I tried looking daughterly, whatever that was, straightening my spine and making sure my elbows weren't on the table.

We smiled warmly at each other and Stacy's mom removed her hand from mine. She stood up and headed into the kitchen.

"Well, we're having roast beef and potatoes for dinner. Go get washed up and we'll have a nice meal."

"Do you need any help, Mrs. O'Connor?"

"Oh, no, you go ahead. I'll call you down when we're ready to eat."

I left the pad where it had sat between us, and went to go smell my new sheets.

In the early evenings, Frank and I hung out in a side room by the garage and he gave me cigarettes while we "shot the shit," which usually meant talking about deer hunting and taxidermy while sitting next to a freezer full of animals that Frank had killed, all gingerly wrapped in brown paper and plastic. Frank was adamant that he used all parts of the animals he shot.

"If you're gonna kill it, you better eat it," he would say.

Once Frank let me hold an unloaded gun. He checked it for bullets three times before he gave it to me. It was heavy, and I laid it across my lap because I was too afraid to cock it and place it over my shoulder. I couldn't hold it for long. Knowing the gun had killed a deer made me queasy.

"Shit," I said, handing the gun back to him.

"Yeah, I know, right?" Frank said.

The room off the garage was one of the places Frank used to go to drink. Stacy told me it had gotten pretty bad, but it was better now that he wasn't drinking. Stacy knew about my dad and his drinking, but this was the first time I had heard about Frank's problem. Knowing that we shared a similar backstory gave me comfort. If Stacy could hold her life together under such strained circumstances, maybe I could too.

"Do you think it'll stick?" I asked.

"Who knows," Stacy said.

Frank never talked about his drinking days, but a couple of weeks after I moved in, Stacy and I found an old stash of his homemade beer in the crawl space between her closet and the hallway.

"It looks like ginger ale," I said, picking up one of the green plastic bottles.

"Well, believe me, it's beer," Stacy said.

I tipped the bottle on its head, watching the bubbles rise against the fall of gravity.

"There's a lot of it."

"I know. Do you want it?"

"Aren't you going to drink them?" I asked. The idea that someone would have access to a hidden stash of beer and not drink it felt like lunacy to me.

Stacy's eyes glazed over as she looked at all the bottles. "I'm not a big drinker," she said. "Someone should drink them."

The beers were fizzy and light, and that was the kind of buzz they gave me. My body would get fizzy. My head would get light. It was a dreamy feeling of being lost in sensation and I took to drinking them whenever I could.

The mattress Stacy's parents had set up for me was comfortable, and right away I slept deeper than I had in a long time. But Stacy was a light sleeper, and I would wake her up every night from talking in my sleep, something that I had been doing since I was a little girl.

Once, I woke up yelling, "Stacy, Stacy, the polar bear on the roof is losing it in the snow!"

Every time I talked, Stacy would report back in the morning, "You said some crazy shit in your sleep," and tell me whatever she remembered. The routine bonded us.

Stacy liked my sleep-talking, because it reminded her of her friend Maya, a girl our age that she'd met the summer before while on a family camping trip. The two of them would have sleepovers, and Maya would toss and turn all night. When Stacy asked her about it, Maya told her that she had just come back from a juvenile asylum, where the nurses had made her take a lot of sleeping meds. Her parents had sent her away after they read her diary and found out she was having sex. When they couldn't stop her from seeing the guy she was having sex with, they'd had her committed.

I hadn't realized it was possible to send your kid away for loving someone you didn't approve of. "All they had to do was pull sections from her diary," Stacy told me. A parent could commit their child for writing thoughts down in a diary. The horror of that revelation sunk in as I mentally mapped out where I had put my journals.

"Maybe it wouldn't be so bad, if you weren't given meds that made you catatonic," Stacy pondered. "It would be a chance to think."

An image of Stacy sitting by a barred window in a juvenile asylum flashed in my mind, the silence of lights out, having nothing to do but think. It didn't appeal to me.

"I need a break from everything," she said.

"Yeah," I agreed with her. "Yeah."

On Fridays Mrs. O'Connor would ask, "How's the job search coming?"

"Slow, but good."

"Any prospects?"

"A few. I'm hoping I'll get an interview when I follow up next week."

Mrs. O'Connor would give me a smile and go back to her dinner prep. I would watch her face for a sign, interpreting the slight twitches in her forehead or the upturning of her eyebrows, trying to gauge how much time I had left before she was going to kick me out. I knew it was coming and had known since that night in the kitchen, the legal pad like a divining rod signaling our ending before it even began.

She ended up letting me stay three months, longer than either of us imagined. Staying in school, completing my assignments, going to theater class, writing—this was what I had to do, what I knew would keep me sane and help me get out. And I wanted to be with my friends all the time, to be surrounded by them, share cigarettes and conversations with them. I didn't want a job and I thought I deserved that freedom. I never put out a single resume.

It was April, almost the end of the school year, and Stacy and I were throwing our overnight bags into the back of Abby's car. Garret was sitting in the front seat, and Stacy and I climbed into the back. Stacy and Garret were still friends, and I wanted them all to meet my dad. I also thought a weekend trip to Vancouver would take the edge off the so-called job search. In my carry-on, I had ten beers from the crawl space. Garret and I cracked open two as we pulled out of Stacy's driveway.

On the way, all of us sipped Frank's beer, and soon I was getting that boozy feeling that I loved so much, the feeling that I was beginning to think that I couldn't live without. I was into my third beer when my brain started swerving with the motions of the car, a slow fizzing high that flushed my cheeks and made the world blurry. This was my favorite part of getting drunk, the buzzing that started in the toes and worked its way to the brain, and I clung to the sensation for as long as I could. The buzz was what I wished I could sustain over a whole night, but eventually I would be totally blasted. I wanted the buzz to last forever. I was thinking just that when Abby turned a wide corner and the car flooded with sunlight.

We were blind. The front end of the car was curling itself around a wide turn, and I felt weightless as we headed into it, like I was on a rollercoaster passing through a momentary ray of sunshine. Abby let herself pass into the left lane to get more space.

Suddenly sober, I caught the split-second glint coming off the semi-truck's front window, and saw the silhouette of the driver's face inside the cab. Stacy and I gasped. On instinct, I pushed my hands against the passenger door, trying to shield myself from what looked like an inevitable collision. Out of the corner of my eye, I could see Stacy bent over and covering her head. We were all bracing for impact.

"Whoa, whoa!" Garret was the first one to yell.

Abby was the only one who kept calm. Driving shoeless as always, she swerved the car into the right-hand lane with one graceful sweep of the steering wheel and avoided hitting the truck.

We drove in silence for a few minutes, with nothing to say and the buzz wearing off. Then Garret burst into hysterical laughter.

"Oh fuck, Abby, you have the reflexes of a cat."

Stacy and I were still trying to catch our breath. We tried to recall the blinding light, the semitruck coming out of nowhere, Abby's quick work, and the narrow miss as the truck passed us.

"These beers are ah-mazing," I said, passing another into the front seat. "They get you just relaxed enough to stay calm right before you think you're gonna die."

Great howls of laughter filled the car as we opened another round of Frank's special brew.

Dad was there to pick us up from the ferry, and the five of us piled into his green hatchback. He had moved to Maple Ridge after the divorce, and Kyle had followed close behind. A suburb of Vancouver, Maple Ridge was an hour away from the city, and an easy place to party. Garret called shotgun, and Abby, Stacy, and I sat in the back. We told Dad the story of our near miss and how we thought the beers had saved us.

"It relaxed us enough to stay calm and save ourselves," I said, patting Abby's arm.

"Yeah, that is dumb fucking luck." Garret laughed again.

I opened my bag to see if I could find one last beer hiding underneath my clothes, but couldn't find anything.

"Dad, feel like a drink?"

Dad didn't say anything, but I could see the half-empty Kokanee beer in his coffee holder. Garret had made a joke and was carrying on with Dad. It seemed like he didn't hear me, and I sat back in my seat, wondering how we were going to get more booze. Dad turned up the radio and switched it to an oldies station.

"Next up, Led Zeppelin's 'Tangerine,'" the radio announcer crooned.

"Oh, turn it up, Dad, this is my favorite!" I yelled.

I pulled a Camel out of Dad's pack without asking and lit up, then passed a smoke to Abby as well. I was trying to remember where the liquor stores were near Dad's place, figuring that if we could get Dad in the right mood he would buy us some booze. That's when he pulled into a liquor store parking lot.

"They sell cheap beer here," Dad said. Then he turned to us. "Okay, give me your money. What do you want?"

"Vodka," Garret and I sang out in unison.

"Gin," Abby said.

"I guess I'll drink vodka too," Stacy piped in from the backseat.

"Nice." I nodded at her. We put a wad of cash into Dad's hands and he tucked it into his wallet.

"Stay inside the van and *do not* come out for any reason," Dad warned us. We slunk down in our seats as he left the van, cracking the window for a little air, watching and waiting for him to come back.

A few minutes later, Garret was squirming in his seat.

"I gotta piss. Where the fuck is he?"

"He's gotta get a ton of booze, Garret, give him some time."

"Yeah, but my buzz is wearing off," Garret whined.

"Give it a minute," I said.

"I could run in there and piss and be right back out," he said.

"No way. You're not gonna bust my dad because you have to take a piss."

"I have to go."

"For Christ's sake, give it a minute . . ." I trailed off. My buzz was wearing off too.

Right when Garret couldn't stand it anymore, Dad walked out of the store and toward the van with two large paper bags. Climbing into the truck with a Cheshire grin on his face, he passed one of the paper bags into the back and kept one up front. Inside our bag was a 26er of vodka, a mickey of gin, a few limes, and a two-litre bottle of Coke.

"Right on. Thanks, Dad."

"Yeah, thanks, Mr. Marquardt," Stacy said.

"I gotta piss."

"Garret," I said.

"Well, it's safe now," Dad said. "Go on inside. Next to the store there's a bar. The washroom's in there."

Garret was already climbing out of the van. "Don't open my booze while I'm gone," he said over his shoulder.

We cracked open the bottles on the road back to Dad's house. By the time we pulled into the driveway, I was well on my way to being blackout drunk.

The rest of the night was hazy. I know we listened to the Rolling Stones album *Let It Bleed* over and over again, and that at one point Garret was yelling at me to stop playing the opening track, "Gimme Shelter." Kyle was at the house, but I don't remember seeing him that night. At one point someone gave me a disposable camera, and I took photos of Dad's tiny kitchen, the ceiling in the living room, and Dad's bedroom, where we all ended up sitting around his CD player. At one point I looked over at Stacy and got her to pose for the photo. She sat up like Queen Elizabeth, her legs crossed at the ankles, her long red hair pulled back into a low ponytail. She was facing sideways and she looked serene, but her eyes were glassy. Stacy was drunk, very drunk, like all of us. Her queenly position was her last attempt at maintaining composure before we all fell into the nothingness of an imminent blackout.

When I opened my eyes I was naked, a translucent white sheet covering my chest. I looked beside me and my father was there. And he was naked. The house was still, calmer than it ever had been, and I reached over and put on my bra. I slipped into my father's walk-in closet and put on one of his button-up shirts, the ones he wore to work, and I looked at him. His jaw was slack and he lay motionless. The air was morbidly stale and humid. I stepped into the hallway, silently closing the door because I didn't want to wake anyone up. I stepped into the guest room and into the bed. I erased the memory of waking up, erased all that happened before, and I didn't even think about what might or might not have happened because I was hungover and drunk. The memory was a haze, where it remained for almost twenty years, until my father called me out of the blue one day in my thirties to ask for my forgiveness for something he said he couldn't remember either.

What was implied in my father's phone call—and what has always been implied in Dad's behavior—was that all should be forgiven, but that it was a courtesy call, since in his mind he doesn't owe me anything.

Years before, when I was twelve, Mom had called me into the kitchen, where they had told me.

"Have a seat," she said, like a doctor about to give bad news to a cancer patient.

Dad looked down at his ashtray as I sat opposite him at the table. There was a horrible silence in the room, and I felt queasy and unsure but didn't know why. Without speaking, Mom and Dad were telling me that something was very wrong, and they avoided making eye contact, so I felt that this horrible thing had to do with me, although it felt like something more than punishment, something deeper and more startling. No matter what they did, they would never be able to take back the words that were about to come out of their mouths.

It was Mom who broke the silence.

"Tanya, we want you to know that you have a father, and that Dad isn't him. Your father lives somewhere else and when you were born, he decided he didn't want to see you." Mom's voice was matter-of-fact, straight to the point. "Do you understand what I'm telling you?"

I tried to put together the pieces of what Mom was saying.

So, my mother is my mother, but my father is not my father. This means my brother is not my full brother, and that my father doesn't ever want to see me.

I nodded at her, though still unsure. Dad looked down at the table, a lit cigarette in his hands.

"Do you have any questions?" Mom asked.

Here again, there was a long silence, but this one was even more complex, about reaching into the past, making sense of a myriad of silences, knowing now why Mom had black hair and I was the only one with blonde, and about the subtle ways Dad treated me as less than my brothers.

I had no questions. I was in shock.

"Can I be excused?" I asked.

Mom nodded, and I went into the basement and sat at an antique sewing machine that Dad had brought home one night, a random present to make up for some drunken outing. I pushed the foot pedal with my feet, the heat from the basement window pouring over my body. The heat was so unbearable that it almost had a sound, slow and methodic, like the rhythm of the foot pedal, pressing and releasing the musculature inside the ancient machinery. It should have matched the beating of my heart, and suddenly the late-night unanswerable pounding and thrashing inside my ribcage had been right. Something was wrong, I didn't belong here. I didn't belong anywhere.

Kyle entered the room and stopped to look at me. I looked at him like I was looking at him for the first time. And though he was just a kid and he didn't know it, he was looking at me for the first time too.

A couple of weeks after we got back from Maple Ridge, Mrs. O'Connor asked me to come sit with her in the kitchen.

"Hon, you and I made a deal. It's been three months, and you haven't found a job."

I didn't say anything.

"Now I know this is going to come as a shock, but I've been talking with your mom the last while, and I don't see why you two are having so much trouble getting along. She's a lovely woman. And she loves you very much."

Mom ruins everything, I thought to myself.

"You can stay with us until the end of the week. Then Frank is going to drive you home."

"Right," I said. "Fine."

"You can come back and visit whenever you like." Mrs. O'Connor reached for my hand. "We're not going anywhere."

"Of course," I said, fighting the urge to flinch and pull my hand away. "Thanks for everything, Mrs. O'Connor."

Although I knew Stacy's mom would eventually ask me to leave, I never imagined she would get in touch with my mom. I felt like they had conspired behind my back. I went and packed my things.

The following weekend, Frank drove me back to Mom and Don's house. I don't remember any long goodbyes. Frank drove in silence the whole time, and I sat facing the window with my eyes closed. I didn't want to watch the world move in reverse back to Don's house.

The causes that led me back to Don's were totally lost on me. Choices that could have served me, like getting a job or talking to my therapist or getting help for my burgeoning alcoholism, weren't on my radar. If they had been I might have understood that loneliness masquerades as anger. As the anger grew into self-entitlement, I didn't think I should have to work, didn't think I should have to get any help. The world had denied me, so why engage in it? I didn't see that I had been sent away from Stacy's because I couldn't pay the rent that I was asked to pay, that I was being asked to leave because I was an alcoholic who stole Frank's liquor stash, a grown man who was trying to be sober, and then gotten his daughter drunk with my father, an active alcoholic. In my mind, I wasn't in any danger. I was the victim of injustice, summing it up as any sixteen-year-old might. They were all a bunch of assholes.

Frank and Mom talked on the back porch. The house was eerily quiet and no one else was home. It seemed everyone had left to avoid the impending storm. All I knew was that I had to drain myself of emotion, become a void that my mother could hurl herself into but find no bottom. She was going to try and spook me, try and illicit an emotional response. It had been six months, and I was back where I'd started, but I wouldn't give her the pleasure of a fight or a crying match. My body was the only thing that had returned. The rest of me was inside, in a dark place that she could never reach.

Frank waved at me before taking the stairs back to his truck, and I didn't wave back, instead going to stand by the kitchen table, not knowing whether to retreat into my room or face whatever was coming.

Mom slammed the porch door shut.

"Tanya, have a seat."

I sat at the kitchen table and looked down at my hands, imagining a tunnel boring itself through the wood into the floor and down into the cement foundation of the house, all the way to the center of the earth.

Mom walked to the head of the table.

"Do you have any idea what you have put me through?"

I was a statue, unmoving. I gave her no response.

"You are *my* daughter and it is *my* responsibility to take care of you. *Do* you know that? How do you think this makes me look in this town? My own daughter taking off like that? People talk. Did you even think how this would make me look?"

Oh, yes, I definitely did think about that, I thought.

Mom paused, waiting for a verbal response. The silence was ripe with expectation. She wanted me to fight, she was showing me that she could take my anger, that she could take my hatred. I wouldn't give her any satisfaction.

"*I am the mother!*" she yelled and then leaning in for effect, she pointed to her chest. "I am the mother and you are the child. From now on you will do what I say."

I huffed but didn't look at her.

"Oh, you think I'm joking? You think I can't take you on?"

I looked at her with dead eyes and gave her a smirk.

"You will not leave this house again. You will live here until you graduate. You will not live with your father. You will not live with your friends. You will finish high school right here, under my supervision."

Her attempt to lay down the law was laughable. I had proven that I could come and go at will, and I scoffed at the idea.

Then Mom leaned in close, her hot breath against my face. I turned my head with a faraway look in my eyes and tried to ignore her.

"If you leave here, I am going to take Jack and put him in foster care."

"What?" I snapped. "You wouldn't."

"Try me, Tanya. Try me. You want to break up this family? You want to see us broken? You run away again, and I'll give you what you want. I'll put Jack in foster care, and you'll never live with him again."

What mothers remember about their teenage daughters and what daughters remember about their mothers often conflicts. The cruelty of what Mom was saying, that she would leverage a child's happiness to trap me, shook me to my core, brought me out of hiding. She doesn't remember saying it and can't imagine herself ever being this cruel. But we could both be cruel, or at least match cruelty for cruelty. And that breaking away that happens in any adolescence, of mothers not wanting to lose daughters, of daughters not knowing how to be themselves and not their mothers, was twisted in our case, residual behavior we were throwing at each other, learned from living with dysfunction for so long. She had traded Kyle, sacrificed him for the possibility of a happier future with Don. But Kyle had gotten what he wanted out of the bargain, and for him living with Dad was a clean trade. And whether she said it, or I read too much subtext into something she said, Jack was an innocent, the only thing that could have kept me in the house.

"That's crazy. You can't do that," I said.

"I will," Mom said, her voice low and serious. She pointed at me, jabbing her finger into my chest. "And if it does happen, if I do send

Jack away, it will be on your head. It will be your fault and you'll have to live with it. Don't test me. Now go unpack your things."

Mom took me to the doctor when I moved back in. Even though I had been fed at Stacy's, the doctor thought I was malnourished and suffering from anxiety. I wasn't sleeping, eating, or shitting. He prescribed an orange-flavored fiber supplement.

"Oh, this'll work," Mom said under her breath when the pharmacist handed her the yellow box. "Your grandfather's on this."

It didn't take long to fall back into the old routine. At Don's I had a warm bed and food, but besides that I had little parental supervision, and soon it felt like I had never run away at all. And after her ultimatum, Mom called the school and canceled my appointments with Mr. Phillips.

"Everything's okay now, why keep seeing him?" Mom said.

I wasn't angry when she canceled the appointments, but I wasn't happy either. I was bone tired and I wanted it all to stop.

Mom acted like I had never run away. She never brought it up around other people and neither did Don or his kids. I didn't talk about it either. Mostly, we sat in the living room and watched sitcoms. I would stare, eyes glued to the screen, not daring to look over at Don's children. I got the impression they were told to stay out of my way, and I was more than happy to be on the outside of whatever secret pact they had made. At dinner, we would sit around the table and actively not talk. Mom would put on an oldies station and dole out pork chops cooked in mushroom soup, first to Don, then the kids, then Jack, then me, and then her.

Mom was only thirty-four. I had no idea who she was, no idea what she was going through. I played like I hated her, but on weekday mornings, while she was in the shower, I would go through her vanity and her jewelry box, not because I wanted to steal anything but because I wanted evidence of her, of who she was underneath the sunny disposition and the constant deference to Don and to all the men that surrounded us. I would touch her fake gold bracelets and the decaying rosary that she got when she was a kid, and the wedding ring she had bought on a whim a few days before she married Dad, trying to locate her true thoughts, her real feelings, which I instinctively felt were hidden in her perfume bottles and gaudy earrings. Sometimes, when Mom would come out of the shower, dressed and ready for work, she would see me looking through her things. She never said anything to me, and seemed to know that I was rooting around for something that she couldn't verbalize.

I adored her. I adore her now as I adored her then, even as we sat at the dinner table in silence, my muscles aching from the strong desire to punch every person in the room, hard, in the face, while "Sherry" by Frankie Valli & the Four Seasons soundtracked our dinner.

Still

I was talking to a group of friends at one of Garret's basement parties, back when I was still staying with Liz and Kristian, when Garrett motioned me over to where he sat with a long-limbed boy.

"Sit down," Garret told me. "Tanya, this is Lars. Lars, this is Tanya."

"Hi," he said, not making eye contact.

"Hi," I said, not making eye contact either.

We sat together for a couple of hours that first night, and I found out a lot about him. He was eighteen but didn't go to high school and lived out past Sproat Lake. His parents homeschooled him after they had caught him getting drunk with some of his friends when he was in seventh grade.

"They're really strict. My mom hardly lets people come over, and when they do she follows us around. She thinks they're trying to get me to take drugs."

"Wow, that's crazy," I said. "My mom barely knows I'm alive."

I was trying to make a joke, and we both rolled our eyes. Lars's life was the opposite of mine, but hearing him talk about his dysfunctional family made me feel closer to him.

"I sneak out. That's how I met Garret. We've been jamming in his basement with my guitar."

"You play guitar? What kind of music do you like?" I asked.

Lars pointed to his shirt, a Cure band T-shirt.

"Cool," I said, "I like The Cure."

"Yeah, I practice at night, but I can't be too loud. Mom doesn't like the music in the house."

I looked down at his fingers and saw that they were long, like mine, but large and calloused at their tips.

"That's impossible, isn't it?" I asked.

"It has to be silent during the day."

The image of him pressing down on guitar strings, strumming without making sound, was heartbreaking.

Lars's shaggy hair fell into his face. He had a strong jawbone, and his skin was pale, with dark circles under his eyes. His legs and torso were long, and he was sitting cross-legged, his waist lean, and with hunched broad shoulders, like me.

"That sounds horrible," I said, inching my way closer to him.

"She doesn't know I'm at a party." Lars took a sip of his beer. "Or that I still smoke pot and drink. The only life I have is after dark."

I laughed. "That's the only time to have a life. Nobody is thinking of you. Everyone's asleep. Then you can be free."

We smiled at each other through our straggly hair, a look of recognition.

"How many nights a week do you sneak out?" I asked.

"Three or four. I have to wait until my parents are asleep. My mom comes and checks in on me around midnight, to make sure I'm in bed. They sleep next to my room, and when I hear my mom snoring, I climb out my window, then push the car up the driveway and down the road until I'm sure they won't hear me turn on the ignition."

"How long do you have to push the car?" I asked.

"Ten minutes, maybe longer. It's pretty dead out where I am."

Now I was fascinated.

"And they don't hear you when you come back?"

"I do the same thing when I come back. Usually it's around three in the morning. I turn off the car and push it back into the driveway. Plus, if I think it's too early, I'll just sleep for an hour or so in the car. I leave a blanket in the backseat for driving around at night. And I stash clothes inside the car so I can change in case I need to."

"You're like a gypsy," I said.

"Yeah," he said, grinning a wolf's grin, showing me his large teeth.

I was like him, traumatized and secretive, and I thought he might understand the part of me that sought out pleasure and danger in equal parts. The idea of finding a counterpoint pulled me in and I clung to him immediately. The relationship progressed quickly after that. In the first month, we went from phone conversations to make-out sessions on Liz and Kristian's couch. I never liked kissing him, though I always thought that I should. His tongue was too big, and when he pushed it into my mouth, my first reaction was to spit it out. But I never stopped him. I figured that was what kissing was supposed to feel like. At the end of that month, we slipped out of another party at Garret's and parked near the local ice-cream parlor, down a side road near the highway.

"I know a place," Lars had said at the party in between hard kisses.

It never occurred to me that when Lars said he "knew a place," that meant he had parked there with other girls. I was too nervous and it went right over my head.

Down that side road near the highway, I let Lars touch my breast under my shirt and my bra, skin on skin. I had made the decision before we met at the party, one-upping myself, trying to push against my own resistance. His hand was cold and clammy, our breath the only source of heat. Lars squeezed my flesh mechanically, *squeeze, release, squeeze, release*. I didn't like it, but didn't know that I could ask for something else. Lars whispered in my ear, right before we started.

"You're beautiful."

He mumbled it. I guessed that he was trying to be comforting, but it didn't work. It was sort of boring, and what my girlfriends told me guys say when they want to make out. But even with the warning, I flushed, as if I had been waiting my whole life for him to say it.

And so I let him go further than I had planned. His thumb rubbed the seam that ran down the crotch of my jeans, and then I lay limp so that he could dry-hump me. It felt good when he did it, a vibration inside my belly. But it was hard to let that sensation take over, because the jean-on-jean friction was painful, and his stubble rubbed my face raw. We were both six feet tall crammed into the back of a Volkswagen bug, which made it beyond uncomfortable, both of us jostling around in the dark wondering how this game would end.

Before we had made out, before we had ever kissed or parked in his car, I constantly had sex dreams—imagining limbs and pelvic thrusts and the sound of moaning. But the reality of making out in Lars's car felt nothing like the fantasy. It felt like Lars and I were wrestling, careening from one side of the car to the other, each of us vying for the upper hand. That night the rules of our game became clear. I wanted to see how much I could endure. He wanted to see how far I would let him go. It was less a make-out session and more a test of wills.

After we finished wrestling, Lars put a wool blanket over us, and I tried not to itch. There was a hollow pulse beating against my temples. It was quiet, and Lars tried to get me to hold him but I held my arms against my chest.

Lars turned to me.

"Are you a virgin?" he asked.

There was a long pause, and I held my breath because I didn't know what to say. If I said yes, I'd risk looking like I didn't know what I was doing. If I said no, it would look like I didn't like him enough to have sex with him.

"Yes," I said, choosing to tell the truth.

"I knew that," he said. "Garret told me before he introduced us. But I thought he was lying."

"Why would you think he was lying?" I asked.

"Well, not that he was lying," Lars backtracked, "more that maybe you had sex and he didn't know."

When I moved back into Don's house, Lars was allowed to come and visit after everyone else went to bed, a concession I think Mom made to keep me from taking off again. I tried to sleep in shifts to avoid the exhaustion of hanging out with him from three to five a.m. on school nights. It never worked. I was exhausted all the time, still keeping the hours I had when I had run away, still dozing off during the day and complaining of stomach problems.

"My mom wants to see you," Lars said one day. "You have to meet her."

"Oh, is it going to be okay?" I asked.

"No, it'll be weird. But let's just get it over with."

Lars's house looked like something out of "Hansel and Gretel." It loomed over me as he pulled into the driveway. It wasn't really a house, though—it was more like a cabin, with a large thatched roof and ornate wooden trim. Before we left the car, Lars took my hand.

"You ready for this?" he asked.

"Not really," I said.

"Well, she's in there. She's making sausages." Lars sighed, opening the car door.

In the front hall, there was a handmade clock with a tiny red door. It was a German cuckoo clock, the ones with the little dolls that circle around and around on a loop when the hour strikes. Above the tiny red door was a handcrafted canary.

"He makes the coo-coo sound when the clock strikes the hour," Lars told me. He started to walk up the stairs into the main room and a woman's voice boomed down on us.

"Take her for a walk," the voice said in a heavy German accent. "I'm cooking."

"Is that your mom?" I whispered to Lars, genuinely startled.

"Shh." Lars nudged me. "She just needs some time. Do you want to go for a walk on the property?"

"I didn't dress for a walk," I said.

Mrs. Muller's voice boomed down again. "There are jackets and boots by the rack. Get her some socks from the winter box."

Lars went to the wall by the front door where there were wooden pegs, thick and homemade, nailed into the wall. Heavy oversized winter jackets hung off each peg and there was a wooden box underneath full of wool socks.

"Here," Lars said, handing me a wool coat and a man's checkered work shirt. "What's your shoe size?"

"Twelve. I'm sure you won't find anything in my size."

"Here you go." Lars handed me a pair of red-laced work boots made from worn golden leather, knitted mitts, and a hat. Then he bent over the winter box and hurled a pair of wool socks over his shoulder at me. I barely caught them.

"Thank you for the socks," I said. "Are you sure it's okay for me to borrow all this stuff?" The last thing I wanted to do was step on anyone's toes. I was already feeling watched, scrutinized by a woman I hadn't met face-to-face yet.

Mrs. Muller shouted, "The socks will make the boots fit!"

Eager to get out of the house, I slipped on the wool socks, mitts, hat, work boots, and coat. The socks made the boots fit snug against my feet, and even though the shirt and coat hung off me, I could feel warmth against my torso. I was sweating by the time Lars had gotten on all his winter gear too.

We walked outside, crunching our way into the freshly fallen snow. Lars's bootprints were forging a trail and I followed him, fitting my boots inside the prints he was making. It felt strange to be with him in the light of day, and neither one of us knew how to behave. This was our chance to be a couple, meet parents, have an unhurried conversation. No ticking clocks and no middle-of-the-night secret rendezvous. Lars had told his mother that Garret had introduced us at a jam practice, one of the few outings Lars was permitted, and even then, his presence was intermittent. Apparently, we had only spoken by phone after that.

It was true that we only talked by phone. I could barely remember any conversations we had when he was at my place. All we did was make out in his car.

There were no houses besides Lars's cabin, and our steps echoed in the silence of the trees and rolling snow piles. I was curious to know this version of Lars, the son of German farmers, the silent son who looked out of his bedroom into a field of snow. What did he think about all day? What was his life like out here in the middle of nowhere, being homeschooled? Did his mom teach him everything? I was amazed by the seclusion of their property, and couldn't imagine Lars living in such solitude. Lars's shoulders hunched a little as he kept walking, the wind picking up.

"How much property do your parents own?"

"I dunno. Like ten acres," Lars called back to me. "They came from Germany before I was born and bought it cheap. My dad built everything on the property himself. He logs to make money."

I couldn't imagine the kind of work that would go into building a house, let alone all the furniture inside it.

"What does your mom do?"

"She's a housewife. She makes all our food, knits and sews a lot of our clothes. I had to beg them for my Cure shirt. Mom doesn't want to rely on anyone for what we have."

"Why not?"

"She thinks we should be self-sufficient. She believes in the old way of doing things."

I nodded and kept pace but was starting to see that Lars's parents isolated themselves on purpose, afraid that Lars would lose sight of where he came from.

"Is she around all the time?" I asked.

Lars got quiet, the snow crunching underfoot. He looked like a frightened child, and I had never seen him look like that before.

"I'm only allowed to listen to music on low when my homework's done. Late at night I listen, and as long as they can't hear it, they don't say anything. But Mother watches everything I do. It's awful."

It seemed like he was a prisoner in his own house. I wanted to reach out for his hand, but before I could Lars stopped and I bumped into him.

"Look at that," Lars said.

He was pointing at a frozen pond, white and still, with muted light clinging to its icy surface. We stood side by side for a while, watching and listening. I started to put my mittened hands into my pockets, but before I could Lars reached out and took my hand.

"I want to show you something," he said.

Lars started across the snow, pulling me behind him. It seemed like everything was asleep, even the air felt like it was in hibernation, motionless as we moved through its thickness.

Lars pointed. "Here."

In front of us was a large tree, the trunk so dark against the fallen snow that it looked burnt. Small wooden slats had been nailed into it, a makeshift ladder going up to a graying treehouse.

"Let's go up," Lars said. "You go first, and I'll make sure you don't fall."

"Okay," I said, hoping to find out about Lars and his childhood at the top of the ladder.

The toe of my squeaky boot felt wobbly against the ladder, but there was space behind the slats to grab them with my hands, and I held on tight as I pulled myself up onto the landing of the treehouse. Lars gave me a push and I slid across the floor, brushing the snow off the bottom of my boots. A sharp wind blew through the open doorframe, making me shiver. With one long contraction of the muscles in his arms, he lifted himself up to sit on the icy floorboards, then shimmied toward me.

"I only come here in the summer. My dad made it when I was a kid."

"Did you have a boys-only club up here?" I joked.

"A boys club?" Lars looked puzzled.

"Like in *The Little Rascals*?" I asked.

"What are *The Little Rascals*?"

"Nothing. A movie about little kids. Nothing." I pulled my jacket up to hide my face, hoping that I didn't embarrass him with the pop-culture reference.

"Well, I never really hung out with girls when I was little, so I guess I had a boys club. But not on purpose."

I shrugged, downplaying the missed connection.

"Am I the first girl to come up here?" I asked.

"Yes, maybe." Lars thought about it. "Yes, I think you are."

He drew himself close to me and buried his cold nose into my cheek, wrapping his arm around my waist. Even under all his layers, I could feel the heat of his bicep contracting as he pulled me closer.

Every part of me was cold. I could feel my thin bones under the heavy wool jacket as Lars kissed me, his mouth and chilled tongue making me feel sick to my stomach. After a few moments of awkward frenching, Lars went for my zipper and I pulled away.

"What about your parents?" I asked. "They're right inside."

"They can't see anything," Lars whispered, sliding his fingers along my collarbone and pulling me toward him.

Lars's hands were predictable and freezing cold. The wind blew bits of snow all around us as his hand went up my shirt. Grab and squeeze. Grab and squeeze. Hard. Lars was sitting behind me and because he was taller, his weight was pressing down on my shoulders.

Lars's hand slid across my thigh and then thrust down into my pants. I gasped because I had never felt anything so cold against my bare skin. I heard my jeans snap open. Still at an uncomfortable angle, I didn't move to lie down and Lars didn't move to lay me down. Instead his hand went over my pubic bone and into my underwear. I felt my blood rushing, trying to fill my body with warmth, but instead I was flooded with anxiety. I didn't want Lars to put his fingers inside me, so I clamped down with the muscles in my thighs and tried to pull them together. It wasn't enough. Lars used the muscles in his arm to push through all that pressure.

His fingers moved in and out of me, hard and fast. It hurt me. It pinched. But I said nothing. Instead I concentrated on the spaces between the wooden slats. If I squinted, I could see the sky through the tiny opening. It wasn't a blue sky. It was still dull gray. The wind was blowing flecks of snow into the air, and I could feel them stinging against my cheeks as they turned to cold drops of ice water on my face. I couldn't speak. I didn't feel like I could say no, and I tried to behave like a statue, inanimate and still, hoping that this would make him stop. It didn't. His fingers were chafing me, going faster and faster until the motion knocked me off balance. I moved my hands to brace myself from falling over. But instead of finding solid ground, I slipped against the icy floor of the treehouse and fell forward, with Lars toppling onto me.

We sat there for a minute, Lars lying across my back, his fingers still in my pants, his head nestling into my armpit. The whole event took less than ten minutes, and for years I couldn't understand why it kept flashing in my mind, all color removed with only the grayscale of sky and the slats and the outlines of our jackets. It was an act performed by a boy and an act of compliance by a girl who thought that was her job. This is how some of us learn what touching is. Later, when I learned about consent, that a man might ask to simply caress my face with his hands, could run his finger down my spine, could show me that he had a heart that could be locked and opened just like mine, I started to see what a lover is, what a lover does. What happened in that treehouse felt wordless and violent, and normal to me then, the way that men and women were supposed to be with each other.

"We can't be gone long," Lars said.

I looked away from him, but not before watching him wipe his fingers off on the floorboards and put his mittens back on. Then I sat up. Lars came over to me and gave me a kiss.

"I'll help you down," he said.

I quickly zipped up my pants.

"Okay," I said, following him to the ladder.

As we entered the house, I could smell a wood-burning fireplace and the oak of the wood cabin. It made my head spin.

"Did you have a good walk?" Mrs. Muller asked, her voice calling from the kitchen.

"Yes, Mother," Lars called up the stairs.

I started taking off my boots.

"Good. Lars, come here," Mrs. Muller demanded.

"Just give me a second," he said.

Lars had put away all his winter stuff and I nodded at him as he went up the stairs. I heard them mumbling in German. As they talked, Mrs. Muller sounded more and more severe, her voice picking up in volume and pace.

"Come get warm by the fire," I heard Mrs. Muller call down.

Lars and his mother were still speaking in German as I came up the stairs, and I tried to ignore them. What I saw made me feel like I had traveled back in time. The room was open, with a fireplace at one end and a long wooden table with four wooden chairs at the other.

"Go stand by the fire," Mrs. Muller called.

The fire was crackling and I needed the warmth badly, so I walked over and stretched my hands over the flames.

"Ah, ah, good to meet you, good to meet you," said another booming voice.

I turned to see a burly man briskly walking toward me.

"Hello, hello, I am Lars's father," he said, taking both my hands and shaking them.

"Hi," I said, feeling my whole body vibrate from his handshake.

"Cold outside, yes? So good you are inside now."

"Your property is beautiful."

"It's large."

"Yes, it's large."

"Yes. Lars had space to run. We are proud of him."

I saw a huge smile spread across Mr. Muller's face, and it made me smile too. *What a nice man,* I thought to myself.

"Sit at the table," Mrs. Muller called from the kitchen.

Lars's father rolled his eyes jokingly at me and motioned to the table. The smell of sausage and sour vinegar was overwhelming. Lars brought out two baskets of warm bread and butter. He was acting solemn and didn't make eye contact with me as he went back into the kitchen and brought back two large pitchers of milk.

"Hope you're hungry," Mr. Muller said, tucking his napkin into his chambray work shirt. "She can cook good."

"Can you cook?" Mrs. Muller asked. She was standing right behind me, and I didn't want to turn and face her. She doled sauerkraut onto my plate with a large wooden spoon.

"I'd like to. I wish I could, but I'm not very good at it." I tried to give a little laugh, but felt no response from her.

She stood behind me for what felt like a long time. Instinctively, I knew not to turn and look at her, feeling her eyes burning against the back of my head. Lars was sitting across the table from me, looking down at his plate.

"Come sit now." Mr. Muller motioned to the one empty seat, and Mrs. Muller moved to her place at the head of the table, where I could finally look at her.

Mrs. Muller had on wooden clogs, which made a clomping sound as she walked. She was wearing white leggings and purple wool socks, presumably knitted by her, under a simple blue-gray shift that looked like a large, shapeless linen sack. It fell below the knee, almost to her shins. Her calves were as thick as my thighs and solid, like the legs of their handmade oak table. Her eyes narrowed as she surveyed the table. She said something to Lars in German. He went into the kitchen and came back with a plate of sausage and a pot of soup.

"Serve yourselves," she said, motioning to the soup ladle.

Lars passed around the soup and then the sausages.

"It smells amazing," I said.

Everything smelled fatty and full of butter, and I wanted to eat it all but wasn't sure if I was allowed. I watched the portions that Lars and his father put onto their plates and into their bowls and copied them, careful not to spill any of the soup, which was a chicken broth full of meat and potatoes. I started to eat the soup.

Mrs. Muller hissed, "We pray before we eat."

"Oh," I said meekly, returning the spoon to its place on the hand-made napkin.

Everyone held hands. My hands felt small and weak in Lars's parents' hands, and I felt unprepared and underdressed. Lars had turned into an obedient boy, looking down and only speaking when spoken to.

The prayer was in German so I couldn't understand it. I waited for everyone to let go of each other's hands before raising my head.

"Did your mother teach you how to cook?" his mother asked, passing me the bread bowl.

"She tried. She's not much of a cook either." I shrugged, trying to laugh it off.

"She doesn't cook your meals?"

Mrs. Muller was playing at being shocked but was mocking me, and I could tell.

"She does. She cooks all our meals."

"So?"

"She also works, and she takes care of six kids. It's a lot."

For the first time in a long time, I was defensive of my mother. Mrs. Muller hadn't met my mother, and it felt like an attack on womankind, on what was permitted and not permitted, acceptable or not acceptable.

"Hmm . . ." Mrs. Muller scoffed under her breath.

"Your home is beautiful," I said to Mr. Muller, trying to change the subject.

"We made it ourselves," Mrs. Muller answered. "We make everything here. We work hard and make a family."

"Is your clock handmade? The cuckoo clock at the front door?" I gestured toward it with my fork.

"Yes, Lars's father made it," Mrs. Muller answered gruffly.

"Really, that's amazing. It must have taken a long time to make," I said. "My mother has some old dishes and a porcelain bird that my family brought overseas from Europe."

"Where are you from?" Mrs. Muller barked.

"We are Hungarian. Magyar. Most of us were farmers. My mom still makes cabbage rolls and pierogi every once in a while. It's my favorite meal."

I was attempting to cross the bridge, show Lars's mother that we had commonalities.

"That is a Polish dish." Mrs. Muller slurped some of the soup into her mouth.

Mr. Muller smiled awkwardly and started in on his sausages. Lars said nothing. We all finished our soup in silence. With each slurp my rage was building.

"Lars says you want to be an actress?"

I huffed, all patience gone.

"Yes," I said, a definitive statement.

"You can't raise a family and be an actress."

I put down my spoon. Mrs. Muller continued.

"I don't think that's a profession for a respectable woman."

What century are we living in? I thought.

"I disagree." I waited for her response. I was done qualifying, and could clearly see that I had failed her test before I had even arrived at her house.

She gave me a long look through narrow eyes, and then we all finished our meal in silence. There was no dessert.

Later, when I was putting on my shoes to leave, Mrs. Muller came to the door and tossed me a pair of her knitted wool socks. I caught them and looked up at her.

"Take them with you. To keep warm out there."

I had decided on the day that I would lose my virginity, and when the day came, a Friday night in early June, I brought a thin white sheet and a set of pillows from the linen closet and laid them out in the games room, on the ratty couch sitting next to the pool table. I tucked the sheet under the couch cushions because I wanted everything to be cozy.

Lars called before he snuck out of his house, the ringing of the phone jolting me awake.

"I'll be there at three," he said. "See you soon."

"Lars?" I stammered.

We both sat on the line, waiting.

"Yes?" he finally asked.

I hesitated for a second, but then pushed out the words.

"Bring a condom."

"I will," Lars said, his voice resonant and clear. "See you in an hour."

I listened to the silence after he hung up. Then I put the phone back on its receiver.

Now I'm a virgin, I thought, *but in an hour I won't be. I will not be a virgin anymore.*

I went outside for one last smoke.

The whole time I was thinking, *This is the last smoke before I lose my virginity.* I looked up at the sky and thought, *This is the last time I am going to look up at the sky before I lose my virginity. This is the last time I am going to breathe the cold air outside before I lose my virginity. This is the last time I am going to be alone with my thoughts, with myself, before I lose my virginity.*

There was a sense of finality to everything, and the feeling that whatever it was that I was losing, I would never get it back.

I kept running through the advice my friends had given me.

"When he pops your cherry, there's blood and it hurts like a bitch, but then it's over," Abby had said.

"A lot of blood?" I asked.

"Depends," Stacy had told me later that night when I asked her the same question. "Abby shouldn't have told you that."

"I have no idea what I'm doing," I said.

"Of course you don't." Stacy smiled. "You've never had sex before. Look, it's no big deal. I mean, there is some blood, but no more than the last day of your period. And there's some pressure when he first goes in, but then it's over. And after that, you can just get on with it. After that first time, it starts to feel good."

"Like when you and Garret had sex?"

Stacy sighed.

"Yeah, sure. Like when me and Garret had sex."

Lars's headlights flashed into the basement window as he pulled into Don's driveway. I flicked my cigarette into a puddle and walked out to meet him.

"Hey," he whispered.

"Hey," I whispered back.

And then he stepped into my line of vision, and we were face-to-face. I could smell him and thought that we should kiss, but I wasn't sure, so instead I stepped back to open the basement door and let him into the house.

My heart was in my throat. We didn't touch as he passed by me into the basement. I was cold with anticipation.

"I set us up down here," I said, leading the way to the games room.

Lars turned on the light and I passed behind him to sit on the green couch, now covered in pillows, sheets, and a comforter. Lars didn't sit beside me and I didn't motion for him to sit.

"Did you bring it?" I asked.

"Yeah."

"Let me see it."

Lars reached into his back pocket and stepped closer to hand me the condom. I pressed the bubble of air on the package and felt the plastic with my fingers, inspecting it.

"Good," I said, handing it back to him.

Lars sat down next to me.

"Do you want to smoke before?" I asked.

"No, maybe after," Lars said.

"Right," I said.

I was stiff. Lars kissed me.

"Can we keep the lights on?" Lars asked.

"No," I said, slipping between the sheets.

I watched Lars walk over to the light switch, taking him in one last time. He shut the door to the games room.

Flick.

The light was off but the moon was out. Lars's body looked like a shadow as he stepped in front of the window, featureless and silent. I couldn't hear him as he walked toward me and sat on the couch.

This is it. This is it, I repeated to myself.

Lars removed his shirt. I removed mine. Lars took off his pants. I took mine off. I left my bra and my underwear on and threw my clothes in a pile near the pool table. Lars delicately folded his shirt and pants, placing them one on top of the other, and laid them on the floor.

He climbed on top of the couch and I pushed the sheets aside to let him in. Instead of climbing underneath, Lars pulled my legs open and got on top of me. My arms were covering my chest. Lars gently grabbed my wrists and wrapped my arms around him. Then he laid his full weight on me, kissing me hard on the lips. I could feel the beating of his heart. His legs and his chest locked me in place, pressing me against the cushions.

Lars's underwear strained against mine. I didn't want to touch him so I went limp and let him move me. He reached under my body, unsnapped my bra, and pulled it aside. I was glad it was dark, but still felt naked. Lars threw the bra to the ground, and the snaps clicked against the concrete floor. He laid his chest down on me, and for the first time I felt a man's naked chest against mine. The weight wasn't as much as I thought it would be, and I knew I could endure it. Lars nuzzled against my neck, toward my mouth, and we kissed some more. I felt paralyzed and detached, like I was watching what was happening from the window, the moon casting faint white light onto the couch.

The closer we got to having actual sex, the less present I was. I could feel Lars's body, could hear him breathing, but could only register the information. I wasn't able to respond. I felt like my body was dead and that Lars knew that, so he was helping me move my limbs.

After kissing, he took my underwear off. It was mechanical, neither one of us making sound. I registered the feeling of having my legs spread open, the air in the room brushing against my naked skin.

Lars put his fingers inside me and this time it didn't hurt. That went on for a while until his tongue was on me. His saliva was warm but when he pulled away and sat up, all the parts that had been warm felt damp and numb. I brought my hands up and covered my face, listening to the soft cotton sound of Lars removing his underwear and pulling out the condom.

Then I heard the sound of a man putting on a condom for the first time, the stretching and then the snapping of latex. It was horrible and even though I knew Lars wasn't going to hurt me, there was violence in that sound, and I knew that pain was coming. Lars climbed back onto me, opening my wrists as he had done before, and pressed into me, pushing firmly against my insides.

I moaned in pain as he kept pressing, his head turned in the opposite direction to mine. And just at the moment I thought I couldn't stand it, the muscles in my pelvis released and the pain was gone. Lars began pressing himself in and out of my body, his head still turned away, and my body went back to being limp and easily malleable.

The thrusting was surprising but not disturbing. It didn't hurt. It didn't feel good either. It only lasted a few minutes.

"I'm sorry," Lars said, lying down beside me, "I can't. I'm nervous."

He stroked my face and I put my arms around him. I didn't know what to say, and watched the moon peeking out over the tree line. It made me feel solid, like I was coming back to myself, and to my body. We lay in that position until I heard him softly whisper in the dark.

"I'm falling asleep. I can't fall asleep here."

"I know," I said.

"I have to go. I think the sun is going to come up soon."

"You're right," I said.

Lars sat up and reached for his underwear. He put on his clothes as delicately as he had taken them off. I wrapped myself in one of the sheets and sat upright, and bringing my knees into my chest, I watched him get ready to leave.

"You okay?" he asked.

"Uh-huh."

"Okay." Lars leaned over and kissed me before putting his shoes on. "I gotta run," he said and kissed me once more in the dark.

He let himself out and I was left alone, wrapped in my white sheet. I watched his orange-yellow high beams slink off into the darkness and listened to his car until I couldn't hear the sound of his tires against the gravel.

I did it, I thought.

That body, sixteen, an appendix scar above her right hip, the eczema scars covering her legs, zigzagging into scar tissue upon scar tissue, the incision of the razor blade from only months before. My scars wanted to be healed and I thought that sex was the way that I could heal them. That I felt that lonely breaks me from the inside out.

But what terrifies me is the thought that I have yet to uncover all the layers of denial, and that there are layers that still exist, ways that I continue to perpetuate my body as a body meant for another person's use. Whether I am wanting to fuck or have sex, work overtime or go out late, do the dishes for the third night in a row or listen to a friend over coffee, I have to always ask myself, *Do you want this? Is this okay?* And tell myself, *You can say no. If you don't want it, it's okay. Just say no.*

Three weeks later Lars broke up with me. He called and told me his mother said we couldn't see each other anymore. Then he started seeing another girl, who I found out was two years younger than me and not a virgin.

TWO

Falling

Twilight Zone

Hurry the fuck up."

Garret called back to me before passing through the admittance gate of the ferry terminal, his steel boots clomping against the concrete. I pulled a wadded-up ten-dollar bill from my back pocket and slid it through a metal slot to the lady behind the gate. She slipped me a ticket and I ran to catch up with Garret, who did not break his pace for me.

Everyone was staring at him. A young family from Nanaimo with matching sneakers stepped aside as he strode by them, and a dreadlocked hippie couple smoking rolled cigarettes glanced at him as he walked through a set of sliding glass doors. Garret walked like a tiny goth prince, looking down his nose at anyone who dared look at his numerous facial piercings, or the black umbrella that he had unfurled to block the midsummer sun from tanning his pale white skin.

I sat down on a bench next to his backpack, amused at his way of moving through the world, unapologetic for the way he looked, though I did feel like a member of his entourage, the provider of his cigarettes, the listener to his rants. But he was so entertaining that it was a small price to pay. Invitations to travel to Vancouver and stay with Garret's friends were coveted, and I had forty bucks and two packs of smokes for the trip. We were going to stay with Lana, who had moved to the mainland after graduation. Garret knew her more than I did, but I had seen her in the hallway, with her dyed hair and grungy floral dresses. We were also going to try and get into a goth club in downtown Vancouver called the Twilight Zone. All my other friends had gotten in when they had gone to Vancouver, and Garret was always ranting about how awesome it was. I looked down at Garret's overnight bag. It was bursting with clothes—Garret liked to have a few clothing options when going to Vancouver for the weekend. All I had were a couple of T-shirts and a toothbrush, nothing fancy.

"So, who all's going to be there this weekend?" I asked.

"I told you already," Garret said. "Lana, Adam, Miranda, me, and now you."

"And you're sure I'll get into this bar?"

"The Twilight Zone, and it's a club. As long as you don't act all freaked out like you are now."

"Well, I've never been to a club before."

"I told you. Stay with us and nobody will ask you for ID. And if for some reason they do ask you, fake looking for it, say you forgot it at home, and then just take the bus back to Lana's and go to bed."

"I don't know how to do that," I said, my voice rising, "I can't go back home by myself, I've never been to Lana's. I've never taken the bus that late by myself before."

"Seriously, shut it. You are going to be fine. It's one bus. And you'll get in. I've never been turned away and look at me. Do I look nineteen?"

He had a point.

A disembodied voice floated through the speakers, interrupting my thoughts.

"Please have your tickets ready as we prepare to board the five o'clock sailing to Horseshoe Bay, Vancouver."

Garret and I stood up to gather our things as the crowd began to line up single file. The ferry was coming into port and I watched its front gate open like a mouth. I had been taking the ferry for years, ever since Mom had brought us to Port Alberni, and watching it dock reminded me of the rodeo, the bull locked in its holding pen, the sides of the cage mechanically squishing against its ribcage in order to soothe it.

"Tickets, please." A bearded man took our tickets, opened a small iron gate, and we all walked single file into the vessel.

Garret pranced loudly up two sets of stairs, flung open the heavy iron door to the outer deck, and walked straight to a bench in the smoking section of the ship.

A prerecorded announcement started to play through the ferry speakers.

"Welcome aboard BC Ferries, Horseshoe Bay Terminal. Your sailing time is about one hour and forty-five minutes. Please don't stay on the vehicle deck. Come up to the passenger deck and enjoy the many facilities this vessel has to offer. These include . . ."

The announcement continued, but I had heard it so many times that I blocked it out, losing myself in the mountains' reflection off the ocean's surface instead of hearing the foghorn blow as we pulled out of the dock. The rolling lull of the ship and its constant forward motion made me feel at home, the way that any moving vehicle could, a sense of adventure and nostalgia building in me simultaneously, the memories of traveling with my father and the anticipation of new places, new possibilities. Floating on the open sea made sense too. I enjoyed the freedom in it, the wind beginning to tease the strands of hair that fell out of my ponytail, whipping them around my face as I went in search of my lighter. Above deck, the wind made it hard to have long conversations, so Garret and I fell into smoking, the flint of the lighter igniting and passing back and forth between us.

Each time Garret and I were silent, I was struck with my own fear. Though I had traveled and moved a lot in my childhood, I was scared of what might happen in the city and terrified of getting caught underage in a club.

I wondered what Lana's place would look like, and was hoping that the two of us would become closer friends. I admired her and was looking forward to hearing her loud, booming laughter. As a girl who wasn't afraid to take up space, she had clomped up and down the hallways of our school in her Doc Martens, and her hair, cotton-candy pink, accented her facial piercings, two on the corners of her lips and one through her septum. She was alive and full of energy. Lana lived up the road from Don's, and my older stepbrother Wayne had known her since they were kids. When I first moved in, I wondered if they had been friends in childhood. But if they had, all that was gone by the time they went to high school.

One day Wayne and I saw Lana while driving home from school in Wayne's truck.

"Fucking freak," he mumbled as we passed by her.

"Fuck you," I replied, half-joking. "I'd rather be a freak than a fucking redneck."

"In what town?" he smirked, also half-joking, adjusting his ball cap on his head before dropping me off.

I watched him speed away, picking up gravel as he swerved down the driveway in his Ford truck. Though Wayne softened and became more accepting as he aged, at nineteen he was like a peach-fuzzed Marlboro man, a clueless kid playing with the air of what he thought a patriarch would look like, which in his mind looked a lot like an ignorant, violent cowboy, something straight out of that Kevin Bacon *Footloose* movie. The cliché made me shake my head in disbelief at my life and what it had become.

Though Garret knew Lana well it was Sam who brought me face-to-face with her. He was the only person I knew who was openly gay. Tall and long, with slender fingers and translucent skin, Sam had come out in his last year of school, and was then followed by a small band of guys who jeered "faggot" at him when he walked down the hallway between classes wearing midnight-blue nail polish or a flower-print shirt with gold brocade on the collar. Lana was always with Sam and a group of "freaks." They ignored the guys, but were careful to never leave each other alone, banding together in their own group, a tactic of strength in numbers. Being a year younger and also a "freak," I was used to the occasional shove or a side glance, but nothing like what Sam went through. I admired him and I was scared of him. He was strong enough to be who he was and risk getting his ass kicked for it.

Then Sam started wearing dresses to school, grungy dresses like Lana's—maybe even some of them were hers. To me he looked like a punk playing at subverting that cultish-Mormon-girl look, with pink hair and cigarette holders matching his large Doc Martens and ankle-length flower-print dresses that gave him a lot of coverage. The entire town lost it. Jeers turned into death threats. My stepbrother and his friends would drive around in their trucks looking for him. The image of Wayne in a car looking for Sam implied that they wanted to destroy him with their fists, which was unconscionable to me. He became the topic we fought about over "family" dinner.

"It's disgusting. Men don't do that. They just don't, and he better watch out. That shit don't fly here." Wayne heaved more mashed potatoes onto his plate.

"How do you know what men do?" I challenged him. "Sam isn't hurting anybody, he's just being who he is. Why does it matter to you so much anyway?"

"He'll teach other boys that it's okay, and it's not."

"Why not?" I asked.

"Okay, that's enough," Mom interrupted. "But he has a point, Tanya. It isn't right."

The potential for violence, the thickness of it in the air, was palpable and increased by the day. I didn't know how Sam could stand all that hatred being thrown at him, or how every day he would get up, put on a dress, and come back to school. Sam would walk down the hallway with his eyes glossed over. He looked like a warrior going into battle.

A few days after the death threats started, Sam didn't show up for school. There was a hush among my friends, and I was terrified that the intercom would turn on at any moment to tell us that Sam was in the

hospital, or perhaps something worse, more sinister. At lunch Garret
told us all what happened.

"He was expelled from the school indefinitely. 'To protect him,'
the principal said."

Garret paced and spewed out indignations. He was so mad that his
speech slurred from talking so fast.

"This isn't about Sam, it's about their fear. The tolerance they would
have to manifest would make their redneck heads implode. Why does
Sam have to pay for their bullshit?"

The morning after Sam was expelled, Garret came to school in
knee-high boots, black fishnets, a velvet dress, and a cape. His nails were
painted black. They matched his lipstick, and his mascara.

"Let's see what those fuckers do now," he said.

Garret was sent home before first period, suspended for indecency
and provoking violence. And then the principal issued a warning. Any
boy wearing a dress in protest of Sam's expulsion would be suspended
immediately. The day after, three other men came to school in dresses.
They were suspended. And that's when the newspapers showed up.

Reporters descended on the school after last period, trying to talk
to the suspended kids. I was walking out of the back doors toward the
store and saw the cameras set up on the sidewalk, a throng of people
standing around them. Curious but uncertain, I walked on the opposite
side of the street to get a better look and saw Garret grandstanding for
the reporters, gesturing defiantly, a microphone shoved in his face.

At least he's grandstanding for a good cause, I thought.

But I think it had been Lana who called the reporters. The more
attention given to Sam's situation, the more the principal and the town
would be under scrutiny.

The Province ran a front-page story, and later that week it was on
the local news that broadcast across Vancouver Island. Two days later,
Sam's expulsion was lifted and he came back to school. Our principal
slunk around for a few weeks, and the redneck kids with their trucks

moved on to weekend bush parties and half-whispered jeers in the hall-way. It was a bittersweet victory. What Sam had done had brought an awareness and a strength to our group of friends, and to the town. But in many ways, the reporting had ended the conversation and moved us all back into the silence.

When Sam graduated that summer, a group of us drove from the high school to Sproat Lake to celebrate. I was shy and didn't know why I had been included, but I was glad to be with the older kids. We sat around in the early summer evening, the sun at that time of day when it illuminates everything. Lana uncorked a bottle of wine and we passed it around between us, sitting under the trees, all our lips kissing the bottle and therefore each other. We talked and laughed, telling each other where we were going, some of us to college, some to Europe, and others would stay in Port Alberni and make a life there. Lana giggled a lot, open-mouthed, showing off her crooked teeth. Sam was there too. They were beautiful in the light of that sunset, and I remembered them as I watched the water pass under the hull of the ferry, all the way to Vancouver.

Lana was still in her pajamas and wrapped in a blanket on her couch when we arrived at her house, her hourglass figure pressing against the crocheted synthetic fabric. Long swirling tattoos that looked like cresting waves wove themselves along either side of her head, emphasizing her large neon-blue mohawk. She was holding an electric screwdriver and a set of wire clippers. Next to her was a spindle of stainless-steel wire and a basket full of tiny steel rings. Sitting beside her on a short stumpy couch was an intensely skinny man. His flesh hung off him like a loose T-shirt, and he looked like he hadn't eaten in years, his bone-thin arms covered in faded tattoos.

"Hey," he said, his voice strong and clear, "I'm Ray."

"Hey, Ray. I'm Tanya," I muttered back, adjusting the strings on my hoodie and trying to look unfazed by his appearance.

"Hey," he repeated.

"Ray's my roommate. Come on in," Lana said, motioning us to sit on the floor.

"Gimme a smoke." Garret slunk down to sit on the floor and leaned his back against the couch.

"Can I have a smoke too?" asked Ray.

I pulled three Du Mauriers out of my pack and doled them out, sitting next to Garret on the matted carpet. Turning to Lana, I offered her a cigarette.

"Don't smoke, but thanks," she said, picking up her spindle of stainless-steel wire.

A television from the early eighties was nestled in the corner with a manual knob for flipping through the channels. An action movie was on. We smoked in silence and watched it for a while. Grainy bodies galloped through crowded streets, and cars and FBI compounds exploded with fiery vengeance. Occasionally there was a tagline, a "make my day" sound bite that made us all laugh, but mostly we sat in a half daze, inhaling basement heat and cigarette smoke.

Lana was winding wire around her electric screwdriver from the spindle on the floor next to her to make ringlets that she cut into a plastic bin.

"I'm making chain mail," Lana said, noticing me gawking at her. "See this?"

Lana pulled down her T-shirt. Wrapped around her neck was a choker made from the tiny ringlets that looked like body armor.

"Cool," I said.

Lana passed me the plastic bin full of tiny rings, and I noticed the thick calluses along the thumb and pointer fingers of her hands.

"My hands are getting pretty tough from all the cutting."

The tiny rings were clipped and open on one side. I plunged my hand into the bin. The open ends of the cool steel scraped my skin.

"You wanna try?"

"I wouldn't want to mess it up," I said, pulling my hand out of the bin.

"You can't mess it up, it's easy." Lana put the handle of the screwdriver between her thighs. "Here, let me show you."

She wrapped the stainless-steel wire around the base of the screwdriver.

"You have to wrap the wire around the screwdriver a couple of times, or else it will fall off when you start to wind it," Lana said. "Then you just push the on button."

The wire wound up the shaft. Then she turned the screwdriver off and passed it to me.

"Okay," she said. "Now you press the button."

"Really?" I asked.

"This is the easy part. On the weekends I do this for hours. Believe me, there is no way you can fuck this up."

Garret rolled his eyes at me. "Scared of a button?"

I ignored him. "Okay," I said.

"Press down hard." Lana punched the air. "Really give 'er."

I took a breath and pressed the button hard and fast. My hands vibrated as the wire wound up the screwdriver's shaft until it reached the top.

"Good," Lana said. "Pass it over and I'll show you what to do next." She smiled at me as she snapped a few ringlets with the clippers. "This is what the clippers are for," she said as each ringlet fell with a tinkle into the bin. "Now you." She passed me the clippers and the wire ringlet.

I wrapped the clippers around the bottom ringlet and pressed down hard. The ringlet jumped out of the clippers and flew through the air.

"Oh," I gasped as the ringlet leapt onto the carpet.

"I didn't get it at first either. Try both hands," Lana encouraged. "Go ahead, try again."

Wrapping both hands around the clippers, I grunted and pressed down. Suddenly, the ringlet released and *clip,* three ringlets went flying onto the floor.

Lana swept them into the bin.

"Nice. You wanna keep going?" she asked.

"No, thanks," I said, passing the clippers and the wire back to her. "What are you making?"

"A bra and underwear set."

"Oh."

I didn't know how to react, but Garret filled the gap.

"Sounds like it'll be cold against your skin," he said, "but pretty hot."

"It will be." Lana grinned with a *clip, clip.*

I smirked to myself and sprawled out on the basement floor, crossing and uncrossing my legs, letting the action movie take over for a couple of hours. Gunshots and car bombs distracted me from the fact that with each passing hour, we were closer to taking the bus into downtown Vancouver, where I would try to get into a goth bar. As the movie credits started to roll, I saw that Garret was pulling at a velvet cape stuck in his bag.

Lana turned to me.

"Do you have anything to wear?"

"Not really," I admitted.

"I have tons of stuff." She grinned. "Come with me."

Lana motioned to her bedroom, and I followed her down the cavernous hallway to her room, a cramped space with a bed, nightstand, small lamp, and no windows. The walls had been painted the same deep purple as the hallway, and I could see thick, uneven brushstrokes under the soft light. Lana opened her closet and started throwing dresses onto the bed, a whirlwind of cheap red satin, black and purple crushed velvet, see-through nylon, and endless tulle.

"I love corsets," Lana said, hurling a few over her shoulder. "I have a lot of velvet. Do you want to wear something long or short?"

"Long," I blurted out. "Do you think your stuff will fit?"

Lana stood up to look at me, her eyes narrowing, mentally taking my measurements.

"Yeah, totally. That's the great thing about corsets. They make you any shape you want. All you gotta do is pull the strings tight, and then tuck the extra fabric into the corset and pin it. It'll be tight against your chest and nobody will see the difference."

I sat on the bed and sank into the soft folds of Lana's comforter. I wanted to lie back and fall asleep, but I was too anxious and pulled aside layers of tulle and fishnet gloves to find the velvet dresses underneath.

"Those are the two longest dresses. One's black, the other's purple," Lana said. "I bought the purple one a year ago. It might fit you better. My tits are bigger now. Why don't you try it on?"

Lana passed me the dress. It was heavy but the velvet was soft, and the front of the corset was embroidered. Thick black string laced up the front of the bodice. I held it against my body. The hem was well past my shins, practically unheard of for a tall girl like me. I looked at Lana in gratitude. She smiled.

"Once you're ready I can do your hair and makeup." Lana grabbed the black velvet dress. "I think I'll wear this one," she said, casually pulling off her shirt with one hand.

I wasn't expecting Lana to be shirtless, and before I could turn away I saw that her breasts were pierced both horizontally and vertically, her nipples large against her even larger breasts, which bounced out of her shirt to rest on top of her belly. A tattoo that matched the two cresting waves on either side of her head sprawled across her chest from collarbone to collarbone. The symmetry was startling. Lana picked up the black velvet dress, slid it over her head, worked her arms into the transparent sleeves, and wiggled her torso into the corset. The train of the dress touched the floor, covering Lana's legs and hips.

I guess I'm supposed to take off my clothes now, I thought, scratching my gray hoodie.

My dress was heavy and I looked down into it, noticing how empty it was. Lana was dressed and rummaging through a pile of shoes on the floor.

"Where's your bathroom?" I asked, trying to avoid changing in front of her.

"Right across the hall," Lana said, unlacing a pair of black army boots.

I was careful not to let the others see me walk into the bathroom and softly closed the door behind me, releasing the knob in slow motion, like a kid sneaking out of the house.

Turning to the mirror, I saw that the overhead lamp gave my skin the look of stained porcelain, a greenish tint that spread over my face and cast dark shadows under my cheeks. I hated looking at myself in the mirror, at my pointy nose and my lanky height, but ultimately the tomboy part of me didn't really care about that. When I looked at myself in the mirror, I felt like I was looking at an alien body, something out of a science-fiction movie. It wasn't just that I was skinny, the protruding bones of my ribs making a cage for my raised sternum. And it wasn't my arms or my legs, long like the wings of some exotic bird. It was that the image I saw felt disconnected from my thoughts and my feelings, and for a split second I couldn't recognize the mirror image as me. That disconnect frightened me, like my reflection was a confrontation, forcing me to admit how little I was engaging with the life of my body. Though in the end, I was the one in control. I could just turn away from the mirror.

Taking a long, heavy breath, I unzipped my gray hoodie, slid it off my shoulders, and held it in my teeth while I pulled open the button of my jeans and stepped out of each pant leg before removing my shirt. Even though I was alone I felt exposed, and stepped quickly into the dress by thrusting one arm and then the other into the long velvet sleeves and pulling it over my head to drape over my half-naked body. I looked into the mirror and frowned. I was wearing a beautiful but large velvet sack. It was disappointing but not unexpected. Twenty pounds underweight at six feet and a hundred and ten pounds, I felt comfortable in boys' clothes, extra-small white T-shirts, and oversized bell-bottoms from the thrift store.

Maybe if I do up the corset . . . I thought, reaching for the hanging strings.

As I fumbled to pull the strings tight against my torso, fabric bunched between the laces and around my hips, becoming misshapen and bulbous. The dress drooped around my breasts, and instead of large milky cleavage heaving over a tight bodice, there was a teeny white push-up bra under the pretense of cleavage. I shrugged and the dress fell off my shoulders.

What are you doing? I motioned to my reflection. I gathered my clothes off the floor and drew them into my chest.

Peeking out into the hallway, I jumped back into Lana's room. She was rummaging through her purse and stood up as I entered. I looked at her like a wet puppy coming in from the rain. She howled with laughter.

"Oh, Tanya, I wish I had a camera right now." Lana put her hands on her hips and narrowed her eyes. "Let me see what's going on. Put your clothes on the bed for a second."

I did what she asked and the corset fell open. My body stiffened and I nervously began to play with my fingers.

"Ah." Lana nodded, walking over to me. "This will be easy to fix," she said, scanning up and down to look for a solution to the drooping.

Within minutes, she had undone the corset and tucked the excess material into the back of the dress so that the corset was snug against my body.

"Okay, do up the corset and pull it tight," she said.

I pulled down hard on the laces, and the dress stayed in place while I tied them into a double knot.

"Got it?" Lana asked.

"Got it."

Lana walked around me slowly, adjusting the fabric, wiping away stray hairs and fuzz with the back of her hand.

"Your breasts," she mumbled. "They don't fit."

"I know," I said.

Lana touched my arm with a giggle. "You're nervous, aren't you? Don't freak out. I've lent this dress to tons of friends. It's perfect because it covers you up but it's also really beautiful. People wear dresses like this to the Twilight Zone all the time. And to Bettie Page."

I nodded. I wasn't completely sure what Bettie Page was. Garret had said something about it being a sex club, and that Lana went there because she was into kink. I had brushed off his comment as half joke, half truth, but it seemed that he was right.

"You can lower your arms now," Lana said, tucking the rolled material into the top of the corset. "We might have to pin it, but walk around like this for a while and see how it moves. Come upstairs. We can do your makeup and hair where there's more light."

I glanced at myself in the mirror hanging behind Lana's closet door and grinned. Lana had fixed me.

I guess I'm going out after all, I thought, following Lana up the stairs.

Half an hour later, as the last of the sun was painting the rooftops with its orange light, we were on the bus heading downtown and drove by a rundown movie theater with a heart sign out front that read "Fox Theatre." Prominently displayed underneath the sign were the letters *XXX.*

"They show Ron Jeremy movies there," Garret said, pointing to a set of ruby-red curtains behind a ticket booth. "There's a headshot of him behind the counter and it's signed."

"That doesn't mean they show his movies there," Lana said. "It just means he went there."

"Probably jerked off to his own movies. Sicko," Garret joked as the theater fell from view.

"Who's Ron Jeremy?" I asked.

We passed into Chinatown and I noticed a tall, dirty-faced man with long, tangled hair meandering across the road, his face covered in sores and his body rigid like a dead man walking. The only part of him that wasn't stiff was his arms. They flailed around independent of his body, dancing to an offbeat tune. The bus slowed to let him cross, and the bus driver seemed unfazed as he pulled up to the next streetlight.

"The poorest postal code in Canada," Garret said. "You know that insane asylum in New West?" he asked Lana.

"Yeah, they just closed it. Some nights, when I'm coming home from the clubs, I see the craziest people on the bus," Lana said.

"Junkies," Ray piped in. "They don't have the space in the asylum so they cut 'em loose, and they get hooked on heroin since they don't have their antipsych meds anymore."

Ray went back to looking out the window. Though I hadn't read about the asylum closing, I had seen it on the bus into Vancouver, deserted, like a ghost town. I didn't want Ray's story to be true, but it seemed plausible and it made me angry to think about the fallout from that level of bureaucratic abandonment.

Lana pulled at a string hanging next to her window. There was a ringing sound and everyone started to gather their things.

"This is where we're getting off?" My voice cracked.

"This is where we're getting off," Garret repeated.

Lana looked at me and winked. "You don't understand what you're looking at," she said, "but you'll see. Everything is going to be fine."

The bus dropped us into the chaos. I stood behind Lana as she stepped down into the street. I heard the bang of the doors slam shut after we all got off, but didn't turn to watch the bus drive away. I was focusing on Lana's back, ready to latch onto the folds of her dress as we turned off Hastings and onto a side street.

The smell of piss, human shit, and garbage hit me hard, burning my nostrils as we walked by an alleyway. Ray and Garret were walking behind me, and Garret took a long, audible whiff.

"*Ahhhhh,* Blood Alley," he called out. "Gotta love it."

His voice was joking, but I didn't think it was funny and kept my head down. The sidewalk was covered in cigarette butts. Yellow piss water lined the gutters.

Lana stopped at the corner.

"Okay, Tanya, do you see that building across the street? The white one next to that bar?"

I glanced to where she was pointing. It was almost dark and the streetlamps were on. A bar with a large outdoor patio was next to a skinny white building with a blue neon sign that read "Twilight Zone."

Lana turned to us. "That's the club. I know the bouncers, so if we all stick together as a group I'm sure they'll let us in."

Garret gave me a scowl. "Stay calm. I wanna dance tonight."

My heart was beating double time, sending shock waves through my body, and I felt clammy and dizzy. But I did what Lana said and stuck close behind her, with Garret and Ray on either side of me.

You're fine, you're fine, you're fine, I kept repeating, but was shaky and trembling.

We walked up to the entrance of the club. A goth couple stood outside the front door, smoking in matching lace shirts and velvet pants. Standing on either side of the black doors were two heavyset men in white T-shirts. They looked like linebackers.

"Hey, boys," Lana called out. She exploded in laughter and gave one of the men a playful nudge. Their faces lit up.

"Lana!" Man #1 reached out to grab Lana's hand and shook it firmly.

"Nice seeing you." Lana leaned in and kissed him on the cheek.

"Going in?" Man #2 opened the door.

"Thanks." Lana gave Man #2 a little peck as she strode into the darkness.

Garret gave me a slight push from behind, and the bouncers didn't even look at me. Lana had curled my long hair, covered my eyes in liner, and then made herself up as a swarthier version, complete with black lipstick. Both of us clomped along in Lana's big black boots, adjusting our bra straps under our velvet dresses. I felt the whole day of worrying fall away, out onto the street and into the night air. Shell-shocked, I stumbled headlong into the club.

Skinny Puppy was blasting through the speakers, Ogre's dark, turbulent voice and high-pitched screech matching the band's telltale metal-on-metal sound. Garret had been playing them nonstop for months. I didn't own any of their CDs but recognized most of their music from hanging out in his basement. My eyes adjusted to the strobe lights flashing above me and I rushed to catch up to Lana and the others, who were headed for a flight of stairs.

"See," Garret mouthed as I caught up to them, "easy."

Before I could say anything we were at the top of the stairs, where there was a bar and a few couches, with tables and chairs in the far corner. Old black-and-white episodes of *The Twilight Zone* were being projected onto the back wall, some images repeating or slowing down, others rewinding and purposely skipping.

Everything glowed neon blue and the goths were out in full force, sitting in groups and sipping cheap beer. Few were wearing color, the black clothes an unspoken dress code, complete with black eyeliner and lipstick, black steel-toe boots, mohawks or long black hair. But there were finer details. Some had dyed their hair fire-engine red, electric blue, or royal purple. There were people wearing velvet dresses like me, giving me a sense of relief, the knowledge that I would blend into the crowd. And then there were girls in peasant shirts, boys in punky school uniforms, all black army fatigues or cut-off jeans, and band T-shirts. I tried to read everyone's mouth to get a sense of what was being said. There were open smiling mouths, drinking mouths, kissing mouths, black-and-red-lipsticked mouths. I couldn't make out a word. The whole thing felt like a silent movie, not unlike the one playing on the wall, black-and-white bodies in motion, people speaking with no sound coming out.

Garret made a beeline for the bar, where an androgynous bartender was serving drinks. Lana tapped me on the shoulder and motioned for me to sit next to Ray and her on a set of upholstered couches in the center of the room.

It was too loud to talk, so I tracked Garret. The bartender had poured him a cold beer from the tap, the brew mixing the foam into a swirling liquid, then slid it along the bar to Garret, who put a five down on the counter. Garret was smiling, frenetic and alive in a way I had never seen him.

Lana tapped me on the shoulder again. "You wanna beer?" she mouthed.

I shook my head, and she turned back to a couple who had shown up, a woman with blood-red hair and a man in a Victorian lace cravat.

My feet were wiggling around inside my steel-toe boots, wanting to run away and hide. Mercifully, Skinny Puppy faded and David Bowie's "Let's Dance" started, a break from the nonstop car-crash sounds.

"Hey." Garret nudged me, motioning me to come stand next to him at the bar. "You remember Adam?"

I had met him a month before, at one of Garret's parties in Port Alberni. He had been shy and spent the whole night in a corner nursing a beer. At the time, I wondered why Garret had invited him. Adam was in his early twenties, and it didn't look like he was excited by the idea of being surrounded by teenagers. But I found him curious. He was slender with angular cheekbones, snow-white skin, and lips that were violet and feminine.

"Hi," I said.

We looked at each other longer than necessary, each waiting for the other person to say something.

"Adam is DJ'ing tonight," Garret cued me and I nodded in Adam's direction.

"Great set so far," Garret said. "You on a break? Let me buy you a beer. What are you having?"

Adam shrugged. "Doesn't matter."

"Cool." Garret waved over the bartender. Adam and I exchanged another awkward silence.

"When you up next?" Garret asked, passing Adam a bottle of brown ale.

Adam shrugged again.

"Whenever I want to, really. No one's even dancing."

I glanced around. Everyone was standing placidly with drinks in their hands.

"Drones," Garret said, trying to impress Adam. "All they want is the same old shit. Eighties goth and pop rock."

"Where's the dance floor?" I asked.

"There's a whole dance floor a level down, didn't you see it when you came in?" Garret scoffed.

"N-no," I stammered.

Adam was coolly watching our exchange.

"It's downstairs." Garret turned back to Adam. "We'll dance during your next set. Hey, do you think you could play some KMFDM?"

Adam nodded.

"Thanks, man."

Garret gave Adam a bashful grin, and he seemed almost grateful to have gotten Adam's attention. I had never seen Garret be so agreeable, especially when it came to music, and it was strange to watch him looking to someone else for approval.

"How can you be up here when the music is still playing downstairs?" I asked.

"What the fuck are you talking about?" Garret said. "You do know what a fucking CD player is, don't you?"

"Well . . ." I was trying not to swallow my words. "The music keeps switching from one artist to another. Did you just put in a mix tape or burn a CD or something?

Garret gave me a look of death. I slunk into myself, shoulders hunching.

"I'm sorry, I . . ."

Adam saw Garret's reaction and a grin spread across his face.

"No, it's a good question. Come here, I'll show you," Adam said.

Adam leaned his back against the railing beside the bar, facing toward me. I hesitated for a moment but stood next to him and peered over the edge, then inched my way closer to the railing when I was sure I wouldn't fall. Adam slid next to me, the heat from his body near mine.

"Do you see that booth? Down there, opposite side of the room?" Adam whispered into my ear.

"Yes, I see it," I said.

Below was an empty dance floor with a few lone goth kids standing along its perimeter like wallflowers at their senior prom. On the far side was a sound booth filled with equipment. It had a large glass window in front and was illuminated from the inside with dim red light.

"That's my DJ booth. All my gear and my music is in there."

"Oh yeah?"

"Yeah. I have my own board. It's like a computer and I can preplan a few songs at a time. So when I take a break, I program some music and the songs play on their own."

"Cool," I said.

I pulled away from him, uncomfortable with the closeness.

"Yeah, well . . ." Adam smiled. "Gotta go," he said before gracefully sweeping down the stairs.

"See ya," Garret called after him.

Adam walked down the stairs, half-smiling with his hands in his pocket. I watched him walk across the empty dance floor, the goth kids parting to let him pass. Adam took one last sip of his beer and put it on a nearby table, then unlocked the booth, stepped into its faint red glow, and locked the door behind him. He started to press buttons on a large mixing board, bouncing to the music as he slipped a set of earphones over his ears.

I danced in public for the first time that night at the Twilight Zone, to The Cure's "Friday I'm in Love." When the first riff came on I almost squealed, I couldn't believe I recognized the song.

"Come on." Lana grabbed my hand and then Garret's, who was grinning all the way from his guts.

And even though I didn't know what I was doing, and even though I had never been there before, and even though I didn't know anyone or how to dance at all, I let myself be pulled down the stairs and onto the dance floor. I swayed and reached my arms above my head, the velvet sleeves of Lana's dress falling against my skin, and turned in a circle and looked up at the neon-blue light tracking across my face.

And, just like that, I was in love.

The Hungry Eye

I went to the Twilight Zone most weekends after that.

Sometimes Dad would give me some extra money, and I would use that as an excuse to go into the city for a night. Other times Lana would invite me, offering me food and a place to sleep for a couple of days. And after that first night at the club, Adam made me a mixed tape, and used flyers he'd taken from the Twilight Zone for the tape cover.

It was a speedy musical education. I listened to songs like "Beers, Steers, and Queers" by the Revolting Cocks, early Cure (before they were The Cure), and early Nine Inch Nails (before they were Nine Inch Nails). After nights out at the club, I would wander home with Lana and Garret at three o'clock in the morning, in the heat of the summer nights, endlessly smoking while waiting for the #8 Fraser bus back to Lana's house.

The Fraser bus at three a.m. was mayhem, a mix of drunks, druggies, prostitutes ending their day, prostitutes starting their day, transgendered kids with black eyes swaying to the whiskey in their bellies, punks with gelled mohawks yelling at each other, beer flying out of their Pilsner cans, the waving of plastic vodka bottles, skinheads with white laces in their steel toes, down-and-out homeless guys mumbling, "Fuck, fucks, fucking, fucker." Invigorating and totally unpredictable, the bus made us feel like we were on a school trip that had gone wonderfully well and horribly wrong.

Late one night, two young queer girls got off the bus near Fraser and 20th, timidly holding hands as the bus slid to a stop. Their friends goaded them on, laughing.

"Don't get stuck in all that plastic wrap!"

The younger of the two girls, the one with long auburn hair, kissed her girlfriend's cheek. I thought it was romantic, but as the bus pulled away, two dudes yelled out the back windows.

"Suck this, dykes!" they shouted, grabbing their balls and pressing the crotches of their acid-washed jeans against the windowpane.

Lana, Garret, and I turned to face the front, keenly aware that we could be targets while also snickering at the dudes as they calmed down and sat in a bus full of queer kids, goths, and homeless poets. It was surreal.

Any time things got really bad, the bus driver would keep his eyes on the road, ignoring everyone passing around joints, or whatever else we had gotten our hands on, like a bunch of kids in *The Electric Kool-Aid Acid Test*. I was terrified, but after a few weekends in the city with Lana and Garret, I felt more comfortable and started drinking at the clubs. After that I was usually drunk, which curbed my fear and turned it into excitement. Suddenly there was pleasure in the watching, mixed in with the fear of what might happen next. Most of the time, riding the bus was fun the way riding a rollercoaster is fun, laughter pouring out of you from the effect of your body being slammed against the rails, with only the leather-and-steel shoulder guard stopping you from flying off into the sky.

I wrote down everything in my diary, mostly abstract poetry with no references to actual events, poems about werewolves and hunger, blood, hearts laid out on tables, and mouths tearing at flesh.

On Sundays people started going to The Hungry Eye, another bar right around the corner from the Twilight Zone. The club was dingier, the staff balding and cranky, but the music was the same, and so were the DJs and the beer specials.

We would waltz in, all of us smiling at the bouncers.

"I heard this place is owned by the Mafia," Lana, in her purposely torn mesh shirt and chain-mail skirt, would joke as she walked to the coat check, which was manned by an orange-haired girl in pigtails and a heavy PVC corset.

The orange-haired girl would smile. "Hey, Lana."

"Nice corset," Lana would say.

"Thanks. Love the chain mail."

Lana would adjust her chain mail and Garret would saunter up behind us.

"You guys wanna check your stuff?" the girl would ask, pointing to a tip jar.

"Nah, we're good," Garret would say.

"See you later." Lana would wave as we followed Garret up a set of musty, carpeted stairs. She'd sling her canvas bag over her shoulders and giggle to herself.

"She's sexy," Lana would say to me. "Don't you think she's sexy?"

"Lana, you think everyone is sexy."

"I know," Lana would mock sigh. "I know."

There was a very specific way of dancing at a goth bar. Garret described it jokingly as "pulling the apple off the tree."

"First you look very solemn."

Garret stood in the center of Lana's living room and put on his solemn face. His lip piercings folded against his cheeks as he flattened his mouth into a long line.

"Then you must slowly, S-L-O-W-L-Y, look up to see an apple hanging off a tree above your head . . ." Garret looked up.

"Your arms float up." He raised an arm lightly, slow as a sloth's.

"You reach." He spread his fingers as he stretched higher.

"You grab the apple." Garret's fingers wrapped around the apple.

"But you refuse to look at it." He turned away. "You hate the apple . . . so you throw it away." Garret hurled the invisible apple to the ground, turning with the momentum of his pitching arm, his black cape gracefully spinning around with him, making him look like a young vampire prepping for a seduction. I thought it was hilarious, and the sound of my tittering laughter accompanied his comic routine.

Dancing was cued by specific music. A great song could fill the dance floor; a bad song could empty it. Until I could recognize these musical cues, I followed Garret's lead. KMFDM was a definite cue. So were Skinny Puppy, Front 242, and Christian Death. "Bela Lugosi's Dead" by Bauhaus, "Spellbound" by Siouxsie and the Banshees, or "The Funeral Party" by The Cure could get us all going. Even Garret. Then we'd all be slow-motion swaying in the darkness, in and out of the writhing neon strobe lights—nighttime blue, blushing pink, and queenly purple. The light enlarged the darkness, and I felt obscured by it, subsumed into it, awash in velvet and black T-shirts, the long goth dresses cascading across the dirty, sticky floor. Every once in a while a white strobe would pulsate, and the crowd would turn into iridescent flickers, leather collars, the sheen of a boot, the sweep of a well-coiffed mane, black hair flying around the crowd of apple pickers. Though I couldn't have articulated it then, I was starting to learn what love was, in those clubs with Lana, Garret, and Adam, whose love was complicated and unconditional.

According to Garret, there were two types of goths: those who loved industrial music and those who loved goth music. If you were into industrial (Garret), you were more "hard-core" and liked harsher sounds: electronic distortions with dark synthesized vocals and arrhythmic annihilation—the scraping of metal on metal or dialogue stolen from TV shows, movies, political speeches, commercials, and talk shows. Industrial singers distorted their voices to sound monstrous; Ogre's demonic growl, KMFDM's Sascha Konietzko's calm German epithets, and Einstürzende Neubauten's Blixa Bargeld's hoarse moaning all echoed in our teenage ears. On the other hand, if you were more into goth music (me), you liked slow, depressing, sad songs, or late-seventies/early-eighties synth pop—like "Christine" by Siouxsie and the Banshees, anything by Joy Division, "The Safety Dance" by Men Without Hats, and Peter Schilling's "Major Tom (Coming Home)" in either the original German or the English translation.

Garret was my professor when it came to understanding the lyrics. I couldn't translate the German songs, but Garret took pleasure in them, studying them like a scholar getting his PhD in Germanic Studies. I also couldn't make out the hidden meaning behind the cut-and-paste musical compositions—the recorded voices under the clanging of what sounded like garbage trucks, and ripped-off tracks from Stephen King movies.

"Ogre is talking about the military-industrial complex. The continuous urge of the American government to create war. They need it, they can't survive without a fucking combatant. 'Deep Down Trauma Hounds,' that title, it's so fucking on, it's about how we sniff out the violence, create our own trauma."

Nodding, I would put the speaker close to my ear, straining to understand. All I could hear was noise, but Garret knew the words by heart and would recite them to anyone who would listen. Garret couldn't get enough—he could never get enough. He loved an audience, craved an audience.

Whenever I was home, I willfully fell into a catatonic state in front of the downstairs television, lying on the couch on my stomach with my arms folded underneath me, a protective gesture, like a bird with a broken wing hiding in a cave. It was an act of resistance, my nonviolent response to being forced to live at home, and I was still heartbroken from Lars breaking up with me.

Mom loved having me around, even in my withdrawn state. Humming an upbeat Reba McEntire tune, she would bring me fresh popcorn and clear my dinner plates, having ingested her signature psychological cocktail of denial and an aggrandized sense of matriarchal duty. Of course she had been worried about me and had spent days without any idea of where I was or who I was with. She was relieved to have me home, I knew that, and yet her doting made me feel more separate from her, as if she didn't see me. She couldn't understand that I was unhappy at home; she refused to really talk to me, leaving me crumpled-up like unfolded laundry on the couch. It made me lonely, with friends and art my only reprieves.

Ms. Moretti, my tenth-grade theater teacher, could do an amazing impression of Louis Riel's wife, Marguerite Monet Riel. She would reprise the role each spring, when our drama class would perform *The Trial of Louis Riel*—a Canadian play that reenacted the trial and conviction of the Métis leader and freedom fighter—in front of invited history classes. Riel was the leader of a resistance movement that grew out of the mistreatment of First Nations people by the Canadian government, and according to the transcripts of the five-day trial, Riel's wife threw herself into the courtroom screaming, *"Louis! Louis! Non! Non!"* and was removed from the room by force. Riel was found guilty five days into his trail and hanged for treason. Ms. Moretti would really get into it, screaming and yelling in full costume as two fourteen-year-old kids playing mounted police dragged her out of the classroom. My heart would jump when she entered, her legs kicking and her face red from yelling the actual words that Marguerite had said during the trial. The play felt like a séance, like we were dragging out the ghosts of Canadian history and letting them take over our bodies for two hours. Though we all knew that Marguerite's screams fell on deaf ears, and that Riel was charged with treason and hanged, the grief of a wife and a Métis woman fighting against systematic oppression was still palpable.

What struck me about Ms. Moretti's performance wasn't the reenactment, though it is etched into my memory, a powerful lesson about embodiment and commitment for a young actor. It was what happened after she was dragged from the courtroom. The trial-play continued, and since that was Mrs. Riel's only appearance, Ms. Moretti, calm and collected, entered a few moments later, changed back into her contemporary clothes, to watch her students perform the remainder of the play, her short hair brushed, her breathing normal. Not only could she control her emotions, she could totally freak out and then a moment later sit in a chair like nothing happened. To me, this was supernatural. I wanted to have that kind of power, the kind of control where I would be untouchable.

Three months after moving back into Don's place, Ms. Moretti pulled me aside while the other students were rehearsing scenes.

"Do you have any after-school activities today?"

I ran through the images of what that might mean, but I knew that chain-smoking and eating microwaved pizza while watching reruns of *Northern Exposure* weren't it.

"After-school activities?" I asked.

"You know, soccer or piano lessons, things like that."

I nodded, giving the compulsory pause where I was supposed to check the after-school schedule in my head, though I was covering and I'm sure Ms. Moretti knew it.

"*Ahhh*, not that I can think of," I said.

"Oh, great." Ms. Moretti sat up in her chair. "I was hoping you might be able to help out with the senior play. We're doing *Annie* this year."

I perked up. Did she need someone to help direct? Act?

"We need someone to clean out the upstairs costume shop. In a few weeks our costumes are going to be made, and I know there are costumes up there that we can reuse." Ms. Moretti's eyes softened. "Would you want to help organize? Usually I would ask a graduating senior, but I'd really like to loop you into the production."

I swallowed. I didn't know what to say. Ms. Moretti hardly ever bent the rules, and senior productions were meant for senior drama students, who got to choose between directing, playwriting, and acting classes.

"Yes," I answered her. "Yes, absolutely."

"Oh, that's so great," Ms. Moretti sighed. "We need someone so badly. We could use you as many afternoons as you're free, and while you help out, you'd be welcome to come to advanced classes. We have a showcase at the end of the year," she offered. "Maybe you could write or perform something for that?"

"When can I start?" I answered.

The costume shop was an explosion of clothes, a tickle trunk gone wild, spilling over every inch of a small, airless room above the theater. I spent three afternoons a week up there, folding musty-smelling ties, pulling tulle and Raggedy Ann dresses off hangers, and taking stock of the piles covering the floor. At first it was total chaos. I pulled at mounds trying to separate long things from short things, then pants from shirts, and finally jeans from slacks, and work shirts from frilly tops and T-shirts. A system started to emerge, and soon I was marking boxes and color coding for the incoming costume designer, until all there was left to do was sweep the floor and turn off the lights.

There was something about the organizing that started to work its way into my brain, a pleasure in having a task and being given the freedom to execute it in a way that made sense to me. Moving boxes and reshaping broken hangers mercifully began to occupy the part of my brain that had been festering with anxiety. No thoughts would come into my head, no major decisions or revelations were bestowed upon me in that room, and there was a miracle in that, in the simple act of being with myself. Even now, when I imagine that room, I feel instant relaxation, and without Ms. Moretti's gift of a calm place at that time in my life, I'm not sure how things might have turned out. I was seeing what I wanted to become for the first time, but it was a soft transmission, grainy and far away, like the outline of a person's body walking toward you in a blizzard.

Still used to keeping "Kristian hours," I fully embraced my insomnia. The nights started to feel like the day, and the day the night. At night, I wrote. I wrote in a fury of words that took over my body, the torrent of emotion I'd been choking all day gushing out onto the page. When I woke up after too few hours of rest, I could barely recall my own name, crawling out of bed like an ameba. Then I would remember that I had to be in the theater that day, that I had to bring my new writing for Mr. Walecki, that I would be taking another advanced playwriting class with Ms. Moretti. I would come to myself in the form of to-do lists and places I needed to be, and as the world came to me, I could grasp the sensation of my personhood.

At the end of grade eleven, Ms. Moretti put me in the year-end showcase. I had written a monologue that I wanted to perform, and one of the graduating directors helped me rehearse. It was the story of an unnamed political prisoner who was being held in an undisclosed prison cell in an undisclosed location. In the monologue, the woman talks about a hand that feeds stainless-steel plates of food through a slot in her cell door. She knows the hand intimately—its contours, the length of its fingers, the crevices and creases in its skin. She tries to imagine the human that belongs to the hand. *Do they have children? Do they sing to themselves? Are they happy?* As a playwright, I thought this was a wonderful tension, the longing to see another person, the intimacy with one's captor. But then, in all my teenage angst, I decided that the hand would feed her something besides food. It would feed her a loaded gun. The monologue ended with the woman wondering what she should do: Should she give the captor what they wanted and kill herself? Or should she deny them the pleasure, and force them to open the door and face her?

Ms. Moretti didn't question the content, and the director didn't ask me why I wrote it. And they let me perform it, onstage, in front of sheet-metal workers, loggers, school administrators, faculty, the principal, and the parents of all the other kids.

The night of the showcase, I stood in the wings, my heart palpitating.

The stage manager motioned as a gaggle of actors exited the stage and the lights went dim. I could see stagehands setting up my scene: a blank stage, a single chair, a door. And then the lights came up, and the stage manager made a long-arm pitching motion.

"And go."

I entered.

During the performance, the audience was motionless. There was total silence. I was sure that they were shocked and that they would look at me in disgust.

Afterward, Ms. Moretti stood beside me as I came off the stage. She grabbed my hand and squeezed it tightly. I thought she might say something, and when she didn't I looked at her, not sure what her reaction might be. She was looking directly into my eyes.

Bettie Page

O nce school was out, I decided to follow in Garret's footsteps and leave town for a while. Seeing Lars with his new girlfriend, a fifteen-year-old with doe eyes and a pixie cut, made me want to vomit, and for the first month of summer break, I'd been moping around the house mentally rehashing the breakup. I asked Mom if I could go to Dad's for the rest of the summer.

"Would it really make you feel better?" Mom asked.

"I want to be with my friends," I said. "I promise I will always tell Dad where I'm going, and I'll only go into the city on weekends."

Mom was hesitant. "I don't like the idea of you being in the city all by yourself," she said.

"Garret is there for the whole summer. We'll stay together and come back on the ferry before school starts. He's even got a job there," I explained.

Garret had gotten a job at a local sandwich shop so that he could spend the two months of summer vacation in Vancouver, clubbing and dating goth girls. As his tagalong, I would only be there for a month, but it was better than writing depressing long-form poetry and staring out the window for hours on end. And Mom knew that.

"I just want you to feel better," she said, putting her hand on mine.

I smiled and stood up so that I could pull my hand away.

"Thanks, Mom."

That weekend, she dropped me off at the bus depot with enough money for a return ticket, and I rode the Greyhound bus, first to the ferry and then through North Vancouver, passing from one place to another, weaving up steep roads, winding around the driveways of enormous mansions overlooking the sea.

Knowing that I wouldn't be back to Port Alberni for the remainder of the summer was intoxicating. I transferred to public transit and headed for Dad's. What had or hadn't happened when Stacy and I had stayed with him the summer before had been pushed into the farthest reach of my subconscious, and all I knew was that Dad would let me smoke in the house and drink whenever I wanted to, which made his place preferable to Mom's, where I had to account for where I was going and who I would be with.

I spent the bus ride copying down overheard conversations—two lovers whispering in each other's ears, old friends reminiscing on their way to a high school reunion, mothers scolding their children. I was firmly living in a fantasy, but I didn't care. I felt like a female Rimbaud, a vagabond with blue ink stains on my fingers, stealing all the life around me and turning it into poetry.

"Hey, Dad!" I yelled as I opened his front door and ran down the hallway.

Dad had set aside a small room for me, and I threw my backpack into the corner. By this point I was highly skilled at living out of a bag, and could happily disappear for days on end with nothing more than my journal, a toothbrush, and a change of clothes.

Weeknights at Dad's were spent writing grief-stricken teen poetry, smoking cigarettes, and watching old Jim Belushi movies. Dad would make me pizza subs and microwave popcorn. I would pretend that he wasn't passing out on the couch. Sometimes he would wake up on his own, a lit cigarette acting as an alarm clock as it sizzled his skin. Other times I would wake him up, his snoring drowning out the sound of the television. After he went to bed, I would continue to write in my diary for hours, long diatribes about what I had seen on the bus and thoughts that had come to me, stubbing out cigarette after cigarette into Dad's glass ashtray.

On weekends I would stay at Lana's, nursing a hangover after going to the Twilight Zone. Unless someone from Port Alberni came to Vancouver, I stopped hanging out with my old friends, the comings and goings of Stacy and Abby fading like an image in a rearview mirror.

Fridays were goth night at the Twilight Zone, and Sundays were goth night at both Twilight Zone and The Hungry Eye. On the last Saturday of every month, The Hungry Eye would host a fetish party called Bettie Page, a BDSM-inspired evening with a goth flair. The top floor was set up like a regular goth club, not any different than the Twilight Zone. But in the basement there was a dungeon, a space for what Lana told me was called "playing," a combination of light foreplay mixed with spanking and whipping, and other activities that were negotiated through something called "topping" or "bottoming."

Garret and Lana were always talking about Bettie Page, and they told me that Adam would DJ the event sometimes. I tried to avoid the subject altogether, but I knew that Bettie Page was the ultimate test in the game that everyone seemed to be playing, one upping each other through addictive behavior or obsession to see how far down the rabbit hole went and what lay beyond it.

Garret and Lana pressed me for weeks until I agreed to go.

"People who go to goth night go to Bettie Page. You can just dance if you want. The people who want to spank each other go downstairs to the dungeon," Garret said. "You don't have to look at anything if you don't want to."

"I don't know, it seems like a lot," I said.

"We'll all go together," Lana reassured me. "It's not as harsh as you think. It used to be in a warehouse downtown. Back then people played in the same area as they watched. This is more like a party. It's totally different."

"Isn't that where you saw that dude get electrocuted until he came?" Garret asked.

Lana shushed him. "It's really not that bad," she said.

"I don't want to see that stuff," I said.

Garret huffed. "Seriously, I'm getting tired of looking out for you," he said. "Come or don't come. I'm going to take a shower."

"Garret!" Lana yelled after him. "She's only sixteen."

When I finally went, I paid my ten-buck entry fee and ran to the far corner of the bar. I pulled out my cigarettes before my crushed-velvet ass could hit the seat of my chair. Garret, Lana, Adam, and Miranda, Adam's roommate, sat around me, which made me feel safer. No one could see me as long as I sunk low in my seat, and from where I was sitting, I couldn't even see the dance floor.

"Do you want to go downstairs and look? I'll stay with you the whole time," Lana offered.

"No. No. Just don't leave me here by myself."

Lana squeezed my hand.

Garret rolled his eyes at me. "Come on, Tanya, fucking get over it already."

"Garret, calm the fuck down."

Miranda was a woman of few words, but they were always well timed.

The music was mind-numbingly loud, and I wasn't sure who was DJ'ing. All I could make out from my vantage point was a human shadow pressing buttons in the booth under soft yellow light.

Adam seemed oblivious to it all and sat silently smoking and enjoying his night off.

I wore Lana's purple velvet dress, a cape, and long fishnet gloves. You couldn't see my body at all. Not bad. I pulled at the long velvet train covering my boots and smiled at Lana, thankful that she was there with me, that she had gotten me ready again, lining my lips and covering them in deep rouge before getting herself dressed in a see-through fishnet top and PVC hot pants.

Miranda leaned over to me. "Let me buy you an Old Stock. It'll be fine," she said, and left with Garret and Adam to get a drink.

They were gone for a while, and eventually I looked into the crowd and saw them on the dance floor. Lana had an older woman with a blue mohawk sitting in her lap, and they had started making out.

"Hey, I want to go into the basement. You okay if I leave you for a bit?" Lana asked.

"Well . . ." I trailed off.

"Miranda and Adam are out on the dance floor. If you need anything you can grab them." Lana made eye contact with me and smiled. "Okay?"

I smiled nervously.

"Okay."

"I'll be back." Lana squeezed my arm before she disappeared into the crowd with her new girlfriend.

With Lana gone, I tried to concentrate on the music, but it was hard not to notice the people around me. There was a lot of skin, bra and underwear sets, naked people with sandals, military uniforms, a couple of nurses, and some dressed like German SS soldiers. I took a long breath. Lana and Garret had prepped me for this.

Everything is going to be fine, I thought, taking a moment to close my eyes.

KMFDM came blasting through the club, raucous noise amplified with a fast beat, an overpowering rhythm that matched the beating of my heart. I stubbed out a cigarette and immediately lit another. The smoke machine turned on, pouring thick white smoke onto the dance floor, and I felt my eyes starting to tear. Limbs, breasts, and asses came in and out of focus, the speakers blasting distorted noise music into the club.

KMFDM transitioned into a Front Line Assembly tune, something loud and brash, but I wasn't paying any attention to it. Leaning against a pole, I lit a smoke and took long, slow inhalations. My eyes were burning and raw.

"Hey," Miranda said, appearing next to me and putting our beers on the table. "Want to dance?"

My legs were wobbly, even though my back was against the pole.

"No, I'm okay here," I said. "I need a minute."

Miranda walked off and I looked around for Lana, Garret, and Adam. Alone again, I leaned back against the pole and let myself get lost in the sensation of smoking, turning my face up to the swirling lights, searching for a sense of calm in the neon.

"Excuse me, miss?"

I snapped out of my haze and stood up. It was an older woman, maybe early fifties, with a leather cap and whip.

"My wife thinks you're gorgeous."

I stood there staring at her.

"She wanted me to ask you if you wanted to come down into the dungeon and play with us."

She motioned to the bar where her wife was standing looking contented, naked except for a pair of leather chaps and a matching collar.

I took a long beat, standing stock-still, unable to break eye contact. When I finally spoke, my voice was high-pitched and dry.

"No, thank you," I said.

"Well, come find us if you change your mind."

The woman smiled as she took my hand. Very lightly, like a gentleman, she brushed her lips against my knuckles. She left me standing there alone and walked back across the room. I watched as her wife kissed her. The smoke from my cigarette floated into my eyes, making everything foggy around the edges like a scene from a film noir.

Lana's chain-mail hobby started to be more than a hobby. She still made chain mail for herself. She rigged up a bust of her own torso and hips by tightly wrapping cling wrap around herself, then gray duct tape, before cutting herself out. It was an impressive fix.

"Those real busts are a couple hundred dollars at least. This is much better," Lana said, reinforcing the inside of her bust with more tape.

Soon Lana had a couple of necklaces, a bra, a vest, a garter belt, and a skirt. She wore them to the clubs, where she got a lot of compliments and started giving personalized friendship bracelets or full armbands to friends and various lovers. When Lana started getting requests for shirts, skirts, and garter belts, she realized she could charge for her work. She tried out new chain-mail patterns on herself before making larger commissioned pieces. Anytime she wasn't at the club, she was clipping and interconnecting ringlets until she had finished a new outfit or a piece of jewelry.

"It looks heavy," I said one day as Lana held up a newly finished chain-mail skirt, "but it's beautiful. You should open a store."

"Everyone's saying that," Lana demurred. "I might. I like making them here though. Just for my friends."

She was standing next to bins of chain-mail ringlets piling up in her bedroom.

"I'd love one of your chain-mail chokers. The wide ones that wrap around your whole neck."

"*Ohhhh*, you'd look great in one of those," Lana cooed. "I'd have to charge you fifty bucks though."

While I saved my money, I watched Lana work on making my choker ringlet by ringlet while we drank chicken noodle soup and chatted, usually on Sunday mornings while everyone else was asleep. Lana was the perfect mix of mama bear and hardcore deviant. After a night of doing any number of sexual things with any number of male or female partners, she could get up at dawn and pass me a steaming bowl of homemade soup, thick from the eggs she dropped into it. My hangover was thankful for the sip of hot fluid. I loved watching the ringlets connect, link by link. Lana could envision the choker from the first click of stainless steel, and I was watching what was in her mind become an object. It only took a couple of weeks to complete.

"I'm gonna wear this everywhere," I said.

I was getting more adventurous, feeling more comfortable, dancing more. One night at Bettie Page, I went out onto the dance floor by myself when I heard the slow lyrics of "Somebody."

"Seriously? Depeche Mode?" Garret called after me.

I turned around and gave him the finger.

The next morning, we were sitting around, hungover, when Garret dared me to go order a sub from the local sandwich shop, wearing nothing but Lana's chain-mail bra and Daisy Duke cut-off shorts.

"You're on," I said.

"I gotta see this."

Garret stubbed out his cigarette and started putting on his sneakers, while Lana did the bra up in the back. My hangover was rattling around inside my head, and my mouth felt like a box of wood chips. The Daisy Dukes were high, tight, and uncomfortable. I looked emaciated in them, my hip bones and ribs jutting out, my pale skin blotchy, my legs covered in eczema scars from when I was a kid. The bra was tight—Lana had made it for a shorter girl, so it made me look flat chested, even androgynous.

"If you're gonna do this, you have to wear platforms," Garret said.

"Pass them over," I dared.

Lana handed me a pair of black leather platform shoes. They had ankle straps, and since I hardly wore women's shoes, I had to sit on the floor and put them on like a three-year-old, folding my leg back so I could reach the straps. I braced myself against a wall and stood up precariously.

"You look like an alien," Ray said through his stoned, half-slit eyes.

"Let's go," I said.

Garret walked three paces behind me as I clomped down to Marine Drive to the sandwich shop. Afternoon customers, mostly seniors, were waiting to get the daily special. I stood in line, hands on hips, black bags under my eyes. I felt triumphant.

Garret was snickering behind me. "Everyone's looking at you."

I glanced sideways at the customers. They were gawking, which gave me more energy. I wanted them to feel uncomfortable, wanted their eyes on me.

"Can I get you something?" the cashier said.

"Yeah, I'll have a pizza sub," I answered nonchalantly, as if I wore chain-mail bras and Daisy Dukes all the time.

"Garret?"

"The tuna fish," he replied.

"And a tuna fish," I demanded.

The cashier quickly assembled our subs. I tossed a wad of small bills onto the table.

"Thanks."

I can't imagine what I looked like. I thought that people were looking at me because I was shocking to them, a slap in the face of their bourgeois morals. And maybe that's partly true. But I think they were also staring because I was young, and because I probably didn't look defiant. I'm pretty certain I looked pale, malnourished, and terrified.

We laughed about it the whole way back to Lana's.

It had been a test. Lana approached me a couple of weekends later while I was manually changing the channels on the downstairs television.

"So, I've been asked to do this fashion show thing."

"It's about time," I said, settling on music videos.

"I know, right? It's totally exciting. I'm going to be showing with this guy who makes leatherwear. It's going to be at Bettie Page this month. Will you come?"

"Of course."

"Would you be in the show?" Lana asked.

I furrowed my brow.

"You're not serious, are you?"

"You're beautiful."

Lana said it like a statement of fact, but I couldn't believe it.

"No way, Lana. No," I answered, going back to changing the channels, an attempt to veer off topic.

Garret was flipping through a *RE/Search* book on the couch, but had been tuned into the conversation the entire time.

"Time to get over your shit, Tanya. I'm wearing a fucking chainmail skirt and I'm gonna be totally shirtless. Man up."

I glared at him, but he had gone back to flipping the pages of his book. Why was he always pushing me?

Lana had an imploring look in her eyes.

"Who's going to be in the show?" I asked.

"All our friends. Miranda, Garret . . ."

Garret raised his hand.

"Adam, and I'll be there too."

I stopped channel-surfing as I felt my cheeks flush.

"What's Adam going to wear?" I asked.

"A skirt like Garret's but a little thinner. I might have them go out together." Lana was baiting me, and I was imagining Garret and Adam on The Hungry Eye dance floor, prancing around like goth ballerinas in their matching steel toes and chain-mail skirts. The image wasn't exactly appealing, but it piqued my interest.

"Is he going to wear a shirt?"

"No, I don't think so. Why, excited?" Lana poked my side.

"No," I lied.

"Yeah right."

I was nervous and started to play with my fingers.

"You know, I am the last person who would ever do this."

Lana knew that I was being genuine, and I could hear my voice quivering. Clomping down to the local deli, half-dressed and in heels, felt like nothing compared to being half-dressed at a fetish party. At the deli I was in control, the patrons' shock a kind of elixir, a way to feel that my body was powerful, mine to wield in any way that I wanted. But at Bettie Page I would be on display, and in the minds of the onlookers, I would be a potential playmate. Everyone at Bettie Page was everyone else's potential playmate, which is why I preferred a dark corner and long velvet dresses. I hadn't yet realized how to say no or that I had the right to control what happened to my body.

Lana reached for my shoulder.

"We are going to protect you, and all you have to do is wear that chain-mail bra. We'll refit it, and I'll put you in a long velvet skirt. And we might get the leather guy to make you a leather collar. Compared to everyone else, you'll be almost completely covered," Lana said.

I knew Lana was trying to be reassuring. And I wanted to participate instead of observe from the sidelines. That's what all the clubbing and the dancing was about—taking small steps. But this felt like a huge leap.

"I don't know."

"Please say you'll think about it?" Lana asked.

Garret was looking at me over Lana's shoulder, giving me the "don't be such a fucking pussy" face.

"Sometimes I really hate you, Garret," I said.

On the night of the fashion show, Lana pulled back the top strands of my hair and let the rest of it fall down my back to give me more coverage. And she hadn't stopped encouraging me since I had agreed to be in the show.

"You have no idea how hot you look right now," she said.

"Really?" My cheeks were burning.

"Don't get nervous. Pretend like you're the hottest girl in the room. We're going out in twos. Enter with Miranda, walk in a circle, then exit." Lana reached out and fixed one of my curls. "You look awesome."

"Hmmm," I said, fiddling with my velvet skirt.

I looked over at Miranda, who was standing near the window, her perfectly olive skin glowing, the light cascading across her face, her green eyes glowing catlike against her smudged mascara.

Why can't I look like her? I thought.

"Thanks," I said, smiling at Lana.

Adam and Garret were in chain-mail skirts, and I tried not to stare at Adam. He was so slender and lovely that I could have wrapped my hands around his waist. The ringlets of chain mail clinked like bells against his legs as he walked.

"You ready, boys?" Lana giggled.

They were both adjusting the sheer black underwear under the chain mail, both of them beautiful and awkward, like young colts at their first race. I couldn't help but laugh because I felt the same way.

"Yeah, yeah, we're ready," Garret answered.

Lana, Miranda, Adam, Garret, and I cabbed to The Hungry Eye. Miranda loaned me a long black jacket to cover my chain-mail bra for the trip. The bra had pinched me all the way to Cambie Street, and I spent the cab ride fighting with the straps, the steel ringlets making their mark against my skin.

After we walked into The Hungry Eye, Lana called over one of the bartenders, who unlocked a storage closet near the back of the club full of beer kegs and bulk rolls of paper towel.

"You can change in there," he said.

Miranda sat on one of the kegs and put her purse on her lap.

"Well, we've hit the big time," she joked.

"Ha-ha, very funny," Lana said, turning to the rest of us. "I have the keys to this closet, so we can hang out until ten minutes before the show. The show is at eleven p.m., and we can store all our stuff back here. The only other people who have keys are the bartender, Eric the leather guy, and John. He makes PVC stuff. Both those guys have models, and they'll store their shit back here too. We're on after John's and Eric's models, so that'll be easy to remember. Go out in pairs. Miranda and Tanya go together, then Garret and Adam, and then Eric, John, and I will come out in costume and do a finale. Then it's over. I'll cue you with the music. Enter, walk in the circle we'll have blocked off for you, go slow and make eye contact. And have fun."

"If you say so," Adam said, adjusting his skirt.

"Where are our beer tickets?" Garret said.

"Oh yeah." Lana reached into her pocket and started doling out two tickets from a long roll. "Each of you gets two beer tickets. I might be able to get more. We'll see at the end of the night."

I am definitely going to need more than two beers to do this, I thought, putting my beer tickets into my bra.

We all lined up at the bar. It was a little before ten o'clock and the club had just opened. People were starting to wander in, but it was still quiet. Adam wasn't DJ'ing that night because he had volunteered to be in the show, and a tall, svelte man in a purple smoking jacket and a tailored white shirt was setting up his equipment in the DJ booth.

We were all served the same light beer, straight from the tap. Miranda and I took our pints to the back deck and lit a couple of cigarettes.

"Have you ever modeled before?" I asked Miranda.

"No. But how hard can it be really? Enter, walk in circle, exit, drink." Miranda took a swig of her beer.

"You nervous?"

"Nah. You?"

I shrugged.

"At least we're doing something. I mean, nothing ever happens at this club. It's so boring." Miranda rolled her eyes.

Miranda never seemed to be into anything. She had a nonchalance that I envied. The men and the women she seduced seemed to love it. The more she acted bored around them, the more they pursued her. I wanted to be like her, to not care about anything and stand around looking like a gothic queen, tall with short purple hair, thick kissable lips, and round in all the right places in fitted velvet dresses.

"Well, you look great," I said. "You always look great."

"This will be so easy." Miranda ignored my compliment. "And after it's done, I'll buy us a beer."

Miranda grabbed my hand and led me back into the club. The dance floor started to fill as the DJ played "Heart of Glass" by Blondie. People filled and emptied the dance floor like they were getting on and off a train, the strobes flashing across the space during entrances and exits. Every time the dance floor filled, there were more people in the club, and that meant we were getting closer to show time. I tried not to think about it, but performance anxiety was starting to take over, my breasts smashing against the chain mail, the bra digging into my chest, making it painful to breathe.

Miranda tapped me on the shoulder.

"It's time," she said, motioning to the DJ booth.

Lana was standing near the booth with a concerned look on her face, waving her arms up and down. Garret and Adam were making their way through the dancing mob. Miranda and I followed them single file until we got to the storage closet and stepped inside. Miranda took off her jacket, whipped out some makeup, and started powdering her face. She was also wearing a chain-mail bra, but her breasts were heaving and milky, like a character in a Jane Austen novel. If we had been in a romantic comedy, I would have been her dorky best friend, the one without any powder and my makeup running down my sweaty, greasy face.

Great, I thought. *Just great.*

I turned away from the other models jammed into the storage closet, bumped into a beer keg, and took a long and painful breath.

You can do this, I thought.

I steadied my fingers and took off my jacket, undoing each plastic button to let the tepid air slip up over my shoulders. Without the jacket I felt naked. Everyone could see me from the waist up. I pulled my long hair across my chest as I turned back around, giving me the illusion of coverage. Some of the girls were naked and seemed fine about it, perky women in thongs standing around smoking cigarettes. One woman was leaning against a wall covered head to toe in a tight purple PVC dress that zipped from the floor all the way up to her neck and connected with her matching PVC facemask. I wasn't standing out. Still, I felt naked and wished I had more beer.

I was expecting so much, wanting to be demure and cold like Miranda, insatiable and intelligent like Garret, get off on the performance of violent acts like Lana. If I could be all those things, then nothing would damage me. I could float above loneliness. I told myself I had to follow through. Anything less would be unforgivable.

Now I try to be tender with my younger self. I see her in that nightclub, full of uncertainty, raw and vulnerable but masking it, wanting to be a grown-up. I wanted to be my own person, and I thought that I was having an adventure, and I was. But I was also a kid standing in a closet without any clothes, and I had no idea what was going on.

Garret and Adam were shirtless, and Adam's chest was thin and muscular, strong and hairless. His arms were smooth but not without definition, his neck long, his legs poking out from under his chain-mail skirt. I was mesmerized by him, and I wanted to tell him but I was too shy. I was about to look away when Adam glanced in my direction and saw how I was looking at him.

His eyes steadied on me.

"Okay, guys." Lana poked her head in. "Get in line."

Everyone shuffled into place. Miranda was ahead of me, and as Adam passed me to stand behind Garret, he put his entire palm on my naked back—his full, open palm, all five fingers, deliberate, cold, and soothing. I had never let anyone touch me that way before and it was electric, my nervous system buzzing in waves. We glanced at each other and exchanged a gentle smile.

We couldn't fit single file in the storage closet, so the front of the line spilled out into the club, where people were being wrangled to encircle the dance floor and make space for the fashion show.

Mistress S., the hostess of the evening, stepped into the open space, a mic in her hand. She was wearing a blonde wig teased to look like Jane Fonda's in *Barbarella*, complete with a PVC bodysuit that plunged down her front, clinging tightly against her large breasts.

"Okay, bitches!" she yelled into the microphone while stepping over the cord in her red pleather platforms. "We've got something special for you tonight. I think you'll recognize the PVC as the work of lovely Jeff, over at Palisades . . ." Mistress S. gave a beat for audience applause before she continued, "And there are two newcomers tonight. We have Eric, with some fucking fantastic leatherwear, and Lana with her new chain-mail creations. It's going to get hot in here. Are you ready?"

The crowd cheered, but in a half-ass way, and Mistress S. stamped her heel and shook her head.

"Oh, come on, are you fucking serious? Give them some real applause."

They went crazy, yelping and clapping over the music, and Mistress S. cued the DJ as she exited, who started playing Einstürzende Neubauten's "Blume (Japanese Version)" on full blast to the cheering crowd.

The first two models entered, a man in black PVC chaps and a neon-blue PVC thong and the woman in the head-to-toe PVC dress. The man was leading the woman around with a leash that attached to one of Eric's leather collars. The woman's head was bowed in subservience and her hands were bound behind her back. They paraded in a circle, the man acting as if he were walking a dog along a promenade, while the crowd swayed to the music. The models did exactly what Lana said they would, walking, posing a couple of times, and then exiting. The crowd loved it.

I craned my neck to talk into Lana's ear.

"Holy shit, you don't expect us to do that, do you?"

"Only if you want to," Lana said. "I'd just dance to the music and see what happens."

Eric's models started coming onstage. They were more conventional—walking, posing, exiting—but it didn't lessen the screams from the crowd. His work was intricate—breastplates dyed in red, blue, and green, with vines and flowers etched into the leather. All of Eric's models were female, and they filled the space with their ruby-red lipstick and strong womanly thighs, the crowd clapping along to the end of Frontline Assembly's "Overkill."

Miranda stepped forward every time a model duo stepped out into the space, until it was just Miranda and me, waiting for our cue.

"Step ahead." Lana inched me forward as Ministry's "Where You At Now?" started to play and two women in red leather miniskirts came prancing off the stage.

Miranda entered confident and sultry, with a hand on her hip. My guts were rolling around in my belly. It was my turn. I was liquefying, dissolving into my anxiety, wanting to turn away and wanting to leap ahead. I took the leap. In the split second it took to step forward onto the dance floor, I decided that the only option was to copy everything that Miranda did.

Putting my hand on my hip, I turned my body to one side of the audience and then the other. All I could see was white teeth and teased black hair. Halfway through her rotation, Miranda twirled in a circle and I copied, allowing myself to be pulled into the momentum of her spin, twirling to the shouting from the crowd.

As I came out of my rotation, I caught the eyes of Mistress S., whose dancing head was at least a foot above the pulsing mob, and she gave me a thumbs-up. Miranda turned again and so did I, revealing the long slit in my skirt and my upper thigh. The swooshing of the velvet teased the hairs on my legs, a soft stroking that sent a tingling up into the rest of my body. Miranda moved to the opposite side of the circle, and as I copied her I heard someone deep in the crowd yell out, "You're beautiful!"

I smiled, copying Miranda's hip tilt, and went to stand by her side. We mirrored each other's neutral "model face," and as we walked off-stage, we passed Garret and Adam, who were entering on the heels of our exit. As we walked away from the crowd, I felt an unfamiliar zing in my bloodstream. *I did it.*

After the show, Adam took me to the dungeon. He told me that he would hold my hand and that if I got scared we could leave.

"Come this way," he said, walking me over to the staircase.

I didn't care about the dungeon. I wanted to hold Adam's hand. His fingers curled into mine, and I felt the goose bumps on my legs as I followed him.

There were two staircases, with people milling around in the shadows, looking at everyone. As we turned down the second staircase, I expected to see the orange-haired coat-check girl and realized it was Mistress S. again, counting out rolls of quarters. She was beyond glamorous. Lana had told me that Mistress S. was transgendered, a word I had never heard before.

Six-foot-four in heels, womanly and gargantuan, Mistress S. could shape-shift in an instant, from man to woman, monarch, hooker, hat-check girl, Cinderella, Cruella de Vil, lady-in-waiting, and torturer. At each Bettie Page she would wear a historically themed costume, ranging from Paris in the 1930s (long ivory cigarette holder and smoldering glances across crowded rooms), Britain's 1970s new wave punk (PVC, wigs of every imaginable color—purple, orange, red, yellow, jet black, and her signature platinum blonde), Elizabethan era circa 1556 to 1603 (old-school fans, large crinoline under a PVC-looking petticoat, white face and red cheeks just like Queen Elizabeth herself), Japan at the turn of the eighteenth century (complete geisha outfit with riding crop and whip), and the equestrian aesthetics of the royal family (whips of various lengths, some with long flaps at the end, others with frayed leather ends).

Adam squeezed my hand and pulled me aside to let a crowd of the barely dressed pass by us on the staircase, and I could smell Adam's sweat, tart and strong. We shimmied down toward the mass of people at the bottom of the steps, my gaze on our intertwining hands. Once there, Adam and I were stuck at the entrance to the dungeon.

I looked up into the crowd. There was more light in the dungeon than on the main floor, which I thought was strange. The fluorescent lights zigzagged across the floor in hard columns that illuminated the space, giving an angelic glow to all the people and objects in the room. Long wooden X-shaped posts with stainless-steel C rings attached were scattered throughout the dungeon and secured to the floor. On the far side of the room, I could make out a man's bare back. He was bound, his arms tied behind him and his hands dangling from a rope tied to one of the posts. The same rope had been wrapped back through a stainless-steel loop in the leather collar around his neck. The man was being dominated by a much younger man who stood behind him, intermittently hitting him with a paddle and turning to French kiss an older woman while she tugged at her own nipple clamps.

Crowds gathered around various scenes, groups of onlookers blocking the stairs and the areas meant for passing from one scene to the next, making it hard to walk around.

The live-action element, the proximity of players to watchers, and the intimacy of seeing someone's vulnerabilities on display seemed to heighten everyone's arousal. This thought made me less afraid. It was all a performance really.

Adam turned to me. "You okay?" he asked.

I nodded. I liked that he cared, that my being okay meant something to him.

Adam led the way as we stepped into the crowd. I was trying not to bump into anyone, but it was difficult, and I could feel the slick sweat of anonymous chests and shoulders as we made our way through the heaving mass. The exposed flesh was red and swelling, but not breaking. Everyone was skilled and using serious tools—cat-o'-nine-tails, paddles, whips, and canes—but with the aim to bruise and blister without drawing blood. I shimmied a little closer to Adam as we moved forward.

Adam had told me a few weeks earlier that he didn't play and only came to the parties because of the music.

"They're a buncha wankers, but it's good for a laugh," Adam had said.

Knowing Adam's viewpoint made me feel safe. He wouldn't try anything with me.

"Do you want to keep going?" Adam asked.

"Sure." I tried to sound noncommittal, but I didn't want anyone to talk to us, or worse, to ask us to play.

We circled around and Adam brought us back to the stairs, where we stopped for a moment to watch a man on all fours, yelping in pain with a woman standing a few feet back from her perceived captive, swatting at him with a whip.

Shocked, I brought my hand to my lips. Adam saw this and he squeezed my palm.

"It's okay," he whispered in my ear. "She won't hurt him."

We all stumbled home together, shoving ourselves into a tiny red car owned by Lana's friend Danielle, who was the spitting image of Robert Smith from The Cure. I instantly regretted getting into her car when she starting driving like a madman, running lights and narrowly missing other vehicles. Lana and Adam had opted for the seatbelts, but I was sitting in Lana's lap, her arms wrapped around me in the illusion of safety. With each near impact I could feel Lana's arm bones, her tendons becoming taut as we made U-turns in and out of oncoming traffic. I wanted Danielle to pull over so that I could get out, but she was dropping off a couple from Eric's crew in a neighborhood I didn't recognize, I had no cab fare, and the buses had stopped running.

"Could you slow down?" I mumbled into the front seat. "This is really scaring me."

Danielle started laughing manically. Her laugh was so cartoonish I thought she might be joking, but then we ran through another red light. At minimum, she was pretty wasted. But more than that, it felt like I was in a car with someone who had a death wish. Lana and Garret tried to soothe me.

"There are barely any cars." Garret poked me. "Have some fun."

The car lurched forward and everyone laughed, while I stared at Garret with a look that said "screw you." Pushing against the ceiling with my hands, I braced my body for what I felt would be an inevitable impact at the mercy of someone who either was too drunk to care about the consequences, or worse, didn't care who she had brought along on her joyride to the underworld.

I was shaky when we got to Lana's. The car hurtled us down the hill to her place and then screeched to a stop outside her front door. Clambering over Garret, I opened the passenger door and went directly inside the house, where I drank three glasses of cool water, leaving everyone to deal with hauling in the bags, my passive-aggressive move in response to their not pushing Danielle to slow down. As I washed the makeup off my face and changed into a T-shirt and jeans, I wondered why I couldn't just shut off the part of my brain that sensed danger. I balled up the velvet skirt and shoved it into my bag, my body releasing the tension from the drive as the night had come to an end. It felt good to get out of costume.

When I came out of the bathroom, I heard laughter coming from Lana's room. Pushing open the door, I saw Lana and Adam lying on top of her covers. Lana had lit candles on her dresser and put a few in glass jars on the floor. Garret was sitting against the far wall, propped against a couple of pillows.

"Oh, sorry," I said, turning to go.

"No, come in," Lana said. "We're just talking about tonight."

I looked for a place to sit, but the only option was the bed, so I sat on the edge, nervous but glad to be alive after riding in Danielle's car.

"You guys were so awesome," Lana said. "And Tanya, I've never seen you like that before."

Lana was leaning back on her elbows and lifted herself up to look me in the eyes. I smiled a little, leaning my head into my hands.

"I'm tired," I said, admitting my exhaustion.

"You should lie down," Adam said.

Before I could respond, Adam put his arm around my waist and scooped me up and over Lana, who rolled onto her side to give me space on the bed.

"Hey!" I laughed, my mind suddenly running through the possible scenarios with Adam. Do I leave? Do I touch him? What if he touches me first? Would I want that? *I'll pretend he isn't here,* I said to myself, and attempted to breathe normally.

I felt like a mummy, lying with my hands crossed over my chest, but fear was replaced by the sensation of gently falling asleep. I forgot where I was and turned onto my side, clasping the blanket with my palm and balling it into a makeshift pillow. That's when Adam put his whole palm against my back, just like he had at the club.

A pulse of heat rippled through my body. I kept my eyes shut, but everything in me was alive in a way that I didn't recognize.

He held his hand over my T-shirt and I gasped, hoping he couldn't feel it.

Just relax, I said to myself. *You want this.*

And my body gave way. I could feel the movement in Adam's palm, the warmth of him seeping into my back. He trailed his hand to my ribs and squeezed a little, rocking me side to side. Lana and Garret kept talking. They couldn't see what was happening. My eyes stayed closed and I let him touch me—and I wasn't afraid.

Then Adam slipped his palm down my ribcage. He traced the bottom edge of my T-shirt and the electric space between the shirt's edge and my jeans. It was such a small space, no thicker than the tip of Adam's pointer finger. I felt like his fingerprint was leaving its mark on my skin. And I wanted that, for his mark to be on me. No one had ever been that way with me; I had never let them. I opened my eyes, and Adam leaned his chin against my shoulder. I turned and we looked at each other the way we had done before, at the club.

"Well, I'm tired." Garret broke the silence. "G'night, guys."

Garret leaned forward, and all of us rolled out of our positions. I sat up. The air was thick in a way I had never felt before, but Garret had broken through it.

"I'll come with you." I scampered over Lana and stood in the doorway next to Garret.

"G'night," I said to everyone.

"G'night," Adam replied.

Any time I was in the city I slept in Adam's bed. Nothing happened. After that night at the fashion show, Lana told him I was sixteen.

"Well, of course she told him," Garret said when I found out. "Hello? You're jailbait."

It was also Lana who suggested I stop sleeping on the futon in her living room.

"I talked with Adam and he said you should just sleep at his place when you come into town. You guys sleep together all the time anyhow."

Lana kept the futon as a guest bed in the corner of her living room, near the crooked green couch. One night I went upstairs to climb under the covers, and Adam was already there, his face pressed against the wall, the light shining against his pale skin. Garret was upstairs and Lana was in the basement, and there was nowhere else to sleep, so I stepped onto the futon to see if Adam would wake up. He reached his arm behind him and pulled back the sheets, staying silent and still to show me that he wasn't going to move. I could see his breath rising and falling, soft and safe, and I stepped inside the covers and lay down. I could feel the small pocket of warmth where his body was, and passed out. The next morning we didn't talk about it. We also didn't talk about it when it happened again the next weekend, or the weekend after that. After a few weekends it became habit and no one ever pressed us for details.

I was embarrassed that I had nothing to tell them. Even after we moved to Adam's futon, I lay rigid with my face pressed against his wall in a half sleep. If Adam shifted at all I would press my entire body into the wall, and woke up feeling like I had slept on the deck of a ship, my neck stiff and crooked. I wondered when he would catch on that I was madly in love with him. I thought that once he did, he would ask me to sleep somewhere else, but he never did, and eventually I could lie in this strange position and sleep comfortably. Adam would sleep on the opposite side of the futon with his back to me and his arms cradling himself, almost at its edge. He didn't touch me.

After that, I started to sleep on my back. He copied me. When I started grade twelve that fall, I was comfortable lying on my side in the same position I did at home in my own bed.

It was Christmas before I let him fall asleep with his hand near me, and well past New Year's before he could put his hand on my hip. Adam waited another couple of months while my body adjusted to his touch, and by the spring we fell asleep spooning, his whole body against mine, skinny, small, and safe.

Early one night, on the futon at Lana's, I had turned to him.

"Adam?" I asked.

"Yeah."

"Have you ever gone out with a girl who's been . . . abused?"

"Yes."

"Did you like them?"

"Of course. I loved them. I've been in love with a lot of girls who've been abused. Too many."

Silence.

"Adam?" I asked again.

"Yeah?"

"You didn't think they were . . . dirty . . . did you?"

"No. No. Never. Not once."

And then we'd looked at each other, straight into each other's faces, and both of us had leaned in at the same time. We put our arms around each other, and we squeezed as hard as we could.

When I was with Lana, Garret, and Adam, it was like I was living in a microcosm, a world hidden within a world hidden within a world—a secret city that kept dark hours and didn't care about daytime life, with all its work and scheduling and monotony. We thought those people were "pleebs" who cared about expensive purses and hair appointments. We were magical and alive—we cared about music and conversation, sex and spit and blood, holding on tight to the space between youth and adulthood. When I look back at that time, my nostalgia can be blinding. Because we weren't night dwellers, vampires who would live forever. We were a bunch of kids playing at being Lost Boys, looking for our version of Neverland by wandering around the city like fools at a Halloween party.

But I was starting to materialize.

One afternoon, I decided it was time for a fresh start and handed Lana's friend Debbie a pair of kitchen scissors.

"Shave it off," I said, tossing my hair back toward her and staring straight ahead.

My hair was long and thin but there was a lot of it, so Debbie braided it to make it easier to cut. She snipped the braid and handed it to me.

It looked like a rat's tail.

"You should keep it," Debbie said, "to remember that you used to have hair."

The plaits of the braid felt thick and seemed to pulsate with the last dying gasps of the person I used to be. I tied the other end of the braid with a hairband I had around my wrist, to prevent it from unraveling. Later on that night, I threw the braid away.

When Dad came to pick me up, I walked out of Debbie's house and watched the color fade from his face.

"Get in the car," he whispered, and then on the ride home he just kept repeating, "What have you done? What have you done?" as if I had done something wrong, as if someone had died.

THREE

Returning

Bait

I was slapping a guy's bare ass with a huge paddle.

I'd had a lit cigarette dangling from my mouth when he had come up to ask me. I was drunk on way too much vodka, slouching against a wall in PVC boy shorts, twenty-hole steel toes, and the chain-mail bra Lana had made for me. He had on leather chaps and was bent over a pool table. Straining his neck to yell at me, he smacked his lips together and words came out, but I couldn't hear anything. He had to ask me three times before I understood. I agreed by lighting a new cigarette with the butt end of the discard, dropping the butt on the bar floor, and stamping it out with my foot. Then I stepped forward, and without thinking, I took the paddle out of his hands.

I strained to remember his face the next day. When I closed my eyes all I could see was the blinding light above the pool table and a sea of formless people beyond. The sound of wood on flesh underscored the din of shouts from the crowd.

Lana, Garret, Miranda, and Adam were in that crowd and they were laughing, a euphoric, almost maniacal laughing. I was laughing too. And it felt great. But I couldn't remember why we were laughing.

The morning after, I woke up at Adam's, too exhausted to go back to Dad's but too hungover to sleep. My head was pounding and I was starving, so I went to the kitchen and found the only edible things in the cupboard. Peanut butter. Honey. Wonder Bread. I pulled out two pieces and scanned the countertop for the toaster.

That's when I saw Adam out on the deck with Tommy. Tommy was Adam's roommate, an anthropology major at Simon Fraser University, a white man with dreadlocks who once opened up to me about his sexual conquests.

"I've only slept with one person," I told him when he'd asked. "How many people have you slept with?"

Tommy thought about it for a long time, for what I thought was too long.

"More than a hundred," he said emphatically.

"Over a hundred?"

"Yep."

"Over a hundred," I repeated to myself in disbelief.

A month later, after eighties night at the club, Tommy and I were inhaling two pepperoni pizza slices when an older, heavyset man approached us with his hands in his pockets. He leaned in toward Tommy.

"Hey, watch out, man," Tommy said.

The older man's voice was barely audible, and at first I thought maybe he was high.

"Excuse me?" Tommy asked.

The older man nodded in my direction. I couldn't make out what he was saying, but Tommy glanced at me in horror.

"Are you fucking serious?"

"I have money." The older man jangled the coins in his pockets.

"Get outta here right now or I am gonna kick your fucking ass."

The older man looked surprised.

"*Now.*" Tommy stood up, and the older man raised his hands in a "don't shoot" gesture and walked away. Tommy sat back down.

"Can you believe that guy?"

"What did he want?" I asked.

"What did he want?" Tommy looked at me incredulously.

I was wiping pepperoni grease from my face and holding onto the counter for support.

"I don't get it."

"Wow, you are drunk. He thought you were a hooker."

"What?"

I looked down at my outfit. My twenty-hole steel-toe boots ran up my leg to just below the knee, and my long black velvet dress was dirty along its bottom edge from dragging on the ground behind me. My dyed black hair was hanging long and straggly in my face, and my black mascara and matching black lipstick were running and smudged from sweating in the club.

"How could that guy think I was a hooker?" I asked.

Tommy shrugged.

We laughed about it the whole way home, but as I stood there slathering peanut butter on my toast, the memory of it disturbed me.

I put my toast down on the plate.

Everything was starting to bleed into everything else. Maybe it was the summer nights with no school and no schedule. Or maybe it was the longer trips to the city, wandering through the streets at three a.m., wondering why in the world everyone was going to sleep when the night had just begun.

It could have been any one of these things, though it was most likely the booze. One moment flowing into another without stopping, experience after experience happening in a state of euphoria, the kind that happens right before a blackout. It helped me to join the game, pushing past my limits with total disregard, embracing the danger even when I was too drunk to know what I was walking into, like hitting a stranger with a paddle. I was invincible. The booze gave me that— potion, elixir, and poison.

On some other night, I couldn't remember when, we were at Bettie Page, and Lana smuggled in vodka mixed with cola in a two-litre plastic bottle. We passed it around, slamming it down so that we could get rid of the booze before anyone could confiscate it. Drinking it burned my throat and churned my guts, but I kept gulping the liquid, taking long hauls off my cigarette in between swigs.

It was when I turned to look at Lana's face that I knew something was wrong. The moment before, I had been drunk, the ever-familiar feeling of flight inside my shoes, the warmth of the booze pumping into my bloodstream, all of us yelling but no one dancing. The music was loud and getting louder—Skinny Puppy's "Spasmolytic" or maybe "Deep Down Trauma Hounds." Whatever it was, it was grating, the iron tin of synthetic noise like a pipe being dragged down to the docks.

And then everything—gesture, music, and language—inexplicably started to lag. Time moved in slow motion, and the music sounded canned and far off, like it was playing in a doctor's waiting room. I could see the muscles in Lana's face, her cheeks and the wrinkling of her brow, the light shaking of her head reverberating through her curls. She smiled, a freight train of a smile that turned into a Cheshire grin. Her teeth looked like fangs. But they also looked like stars, shiny and gleaming from the neon-blue light. They were mesmerizing, almost enchanting, and my eyes were locked on her.

Then her lips parted and she mouthed words in a painful sprawl of strange English.

"SSSSSSSSSSooooooooommmmeone puuuuuut accidddddddd innnn ouuuuur driiink . . ."

Lana giggled, but instead of its usual Betty Boop / Shirley Temple quality, her giggling had the sound of single nails being dropped into a steel bucket. She shook the plastic jug in my face, tracers of color and gesture drifting like a ballet across my line of vision.

My gullet dropped into my gut, and just as suddenly as it had slowed, time sped up to an incredible pitch, a screeching that only encouraged my terror. In what seemed like a matter of seconds, we were all transported into Lana's living room. I had vague notions of being in a car that was moving so fast it was plummeting toward the house, and laughter, hoots and howling, from the gaggle of people surrounding me. It felt like there were a million people in the car, but I could only recognize Lana and Garret. In the living room, the wood paneling on the wall was pulsing, the green carpet blowing like fake grass in an outdoor minigolf course. Lana was still holding the dreaded plastic bottle, and the sight of it made me want to puke.

I loved alcohol, craved alcohol. But I hated drugs. The few times I had smoked pot, I had become incapacitated, lying immobile on the floor while shoveling Oreo cookies into my face before passing out. My friends thought it was great, but I didn't like the idea of losing control of my body. I preferred to be wild with a belly full of booze instead of remembering what happened when I was high and unable to move.

The lights overhead were swaying, and people looked more like sketches of themselves, life-sized moving paper dolls with drawn-in charcoal shadows.

"I can't be here. I can't do this . . ." I said out loud.

No one heard me, but I wasn't trying to talk to anyone. It was my body trying to talk to me. I turned away from the party and Lana walked up beside me.

"You okay?" she asked.

"I need to go lay down. I need to be by myself."

"That's not a good idea. You shouldn't trip by yourself." Lana tried to pull me back toward the party, but I backed away.

"I'll be upstairs. I just need to pass out."

I tumbled toward the stairs to the upper floor, where I knew there would be a quiet bedroom.

Lana hollered after me, "We're here if you need us!"

The bedroom was the epitome of goth, with black carpet, walls, drapes, bedsheets, pillow cases, and clothing. It smelled like lilacs at a funeral. I didn't turn on the light when I stepped inside, and the sound from downstairs fell away as I slowly shut the door. Black. Darkness. The heavy drapes let in only a sliver of white light, and to me it looked like half a cross suspended in midair. I dropped to the floor, not sure if I was kneeling on the futon or the deep shag carpet, lay down in the silence, and stared at the half cross of light. I was overcome with the feeling that some sort of God was present and listening to my prayer for oblivion, my desire to forget where I was.

Was "God" trying to talk to me? Was it the drugs? Whatever it was, it felt real. Even if it wasn't real, it was what I hoped was real— communion with something bigger than myself. I curled onto my side so that I could get a better look, wanting to be bathed in light. It would be years before I would have that feeling without booze or drugs.

At some point I drifted into sleep, the memory of the half cross and stark white light replaced by the feeling of the sun, a warm sliver of orange peeking through the drapery. If I had been on the futon, I had rolled off in the night and a nameless couple had replaced me, crawling under the sheets to fall asleep. I caught a glimpse of their greasy black hair out of the corner of my eye, and heard their light snoring floating into my throbbing eardrums.

Where am I?

This was becoming a more frequent thought, and I put my head in my hands and squeezed until I got an answer, the night before coming in snapshots, enough information to orient myself.

Thirsty, I rolled to standing and crept downstairs for some water. Garret was standing in the kitchen flicking ashes into a beer can as I walked by him on my way to the sink.

"You were so fucked up last night," Garret said.

I barely heard him as I turned on the faucet before making my way to the table. The smoke from Garret's cigarette was making me sick, and I rubbed my eyes with the back of my hand, hoping that I could keep the water down.

"What do you mean?" I asked.

"You don't remember?" he asked, sitting down beside me.

"We barely saw each other last night. We got home, I went upstairs and passed out. I didn't ask to be on acid you know. That freaked me out," I said, fishing for an apology or at least someone else to blame.

"Didn't seem like it when you passed me on the stairs." Garret raised one of his eyebrows.

"What do you mean?"

It felt like it was too early to be talking, but too late in the day to be recalling the events from the night before.

"I was coming down the stairs from the bathroom when you were walking up."

"Yeah, so?" I said.

All I wanted to do was drink my water, a task I was barely accomplishing. Even a small sip of liquid caused a palpitating nausea, an almost incapacitating pain in my belly as I fought the urge to go to the bathroom and make myself throw up.

"You were banging into the walls in the stairway, one side and then the other. You looked, like, totally wild or something."

"I was high, what do you expect." I laughed.

"No, it was different," Garret said. "You were really fucking messed up. I couldn't recognize you."

I looked up at Garret, whose tone was suddenly serious. He was speaking to me in a way that I rarely heard from him. I hated having to hear these frightening stories, having to piece together what I did or didn't do, what I said or didn't say.

"When we passed each other on the staircase, I was sure you were going to fall, and I was about to put out my hands to grab you, but instead you grabbed me, like really fucking hard, and you pushed me against the wall. It hurt."

"What? Come on," I said, brushing him off.

"You really don't remember?"

I shook my head.

"You pushed me against the wall, pinned me, and then you kissed me crazy, French kissed me, but your tongue was all over my face, like a fucking animal or something."

"No way," I scoffed. "I would never do that."

"Well, you did." Garret stubbed out his smoke. "You did it, and I was there. I remember."

She's Lost Control

You're always welcome here, Tanya. You know that," Dad said one night when I asked him if I could stay. Kyle had been living with Dad for well over a year, and he was doing well. He had new friends, he seemed to be enjoying school, and best of all, Dad mostly left us both alone. Now the only problem was Mom. She had let me leave for the summer, but she had also made me promise I would come back. A week before my return date, I got up the nerve to call her.

"So what ferry are you taking back on Sunday?" Mom asked.

"I'm not. I'm not taking a ferry back."

I was repeating what I had said the November before, just using different words on a phone that was farther away, an ocean between us.

"What are you talking about?"

"I'm staying at Dad's," I said stoically. "I'll go to the same school as Kyle, do my last year here, graduate, and then go to college. Dad and I worked it all out."

"Oh, you did, did you?"

I could hear the exhaustion in her voice and hoped I was wearing her down the way that Kyle had before he had moved to the mainland. But I could hear the tremoring in her voice and reached out to console her.

"Yeah. This is going to be better. I'll finish school here and I'll be with Dad. It won't be like before, and I'll come for visits."

"You can't do that," Mom said, anger replacing her sadness.

"You let Kyle."

"That was different. He needed to go. You don't."

"That's not true."

I waited for Mom to admit that I was right and to let me go, that Don's place wasn't the place for me to be and that we would be all right.

"Right." Mom broke the silence. "Well, if your dad said it's okay, and that's what you want, fine."

She sounded reserved but I was dumbfounded. It was not the reaction I had expected.

"It's what I want," I reiterated.

Mom didn't fight. She didn't even scoff.

"There's a place here for you if you change your mind."

"Thanks."

"I love you, Tanya."

Her voice didn't waver, so I didn't let mine waver either, both of us like stones washed smooth beneath a cold river. I knew she wanted me to say that I loved her. I couldn't give her that, perceiving it as a loss of power.

"Talk later," I said, and hung up.

That was easy, I thought.

Dad and I were outside smoking the next morning when a cop car pulled into the driveway, followed by Mom's white four-door minivan. Both cars idled as Mom got out and walked toward us. The cop adjusted his belt as he stepped out of his car. They stood side by side, staring at us. Dad and I stared back, motionless except for the smoke rising from our cigarettes.

The police officer took a step forward.

"Sir, I'm here to discuss a domestic complaint. Your ex-wife says you've taken her daughter without her consent."

Mom's face was fearless and powerful, but she stayed behind the cop, using him as a human shield, and I sensed an invisible dividing line between them and us.

"Tanya, get your stuff. We're leaving right now," Mom called to me.

Dad's shoulders slumped. He looked defeated, like a child who had been caught doing something wrong.

"I'm willing to press charges, Officer. Unless my daughter comes with me, I want you to arrest my ex-husband."

Is this really happening? I thought.

"Mrs. Marquardt says she has the legal right to take her daughter, Mr. Marquardt. Is there going to be a problem?"

The officer tucked his thumbs into his belt.

It felt like I was looking down the barrel of a gun, Dad and I held up without warning. It was shocking and I wanted to disappear completely.

"No, there won't be a problem." Dad turned to me. "Tanya, you better go get your stuff."

Mom nodded to me with a stern look on her face. I looked inside her van and I could see Jack sitting in the front seat.

She can't do this. She can't actually be doing this.

The police officer was looming, and I couldn't help but flashback to the divorce, when Mom had taken us from Nelson, and we had spent an afternoon in the back of a cruiser.

These were the moments that I longed for my biological father, a man I knew little about and wouldn't meet for another ten years. He was mythical, and everything that my family wasn't. Mom hated talking about him.

"Don't look at me like that," she'd told me one afternoon the year before. Both of us were in her bedroom getting ready to drive into town on errands.

"Look at you like what?" I asked.

"You look just like your father when you do that," she said, exiting the bedroom to get her jacket.

"Do what?" I called after her. "Do what?"

But none of that mattered. My biological dad—a man who, I imagined, looked like someone out of a Norman Rockwell painting, with a calm temperament and a houndstooth jacket with "I'm so wise" patches on the elbows—was not coming.

Now that I was eye to eye with a police officer, I wanted to tell him that Mom had given me permission on the phone to stay with Dad, but I didn't have any proof of that, and I knew Mom could probably have Dad arrested if I didn't go with her.

"Give me a minute."

I went into the house and straight down the hallway to my bedroom. Kyle was in his room on the computer, totally oblivious to what was happening outside.

"Mom's here," I said, walking into my room. "I'm leaving."

Kyle opened his blinds and saw the cop car and Mom standing near her van.

"What's going on?" he said.

"I have no idea," I said, throwing clothes into my backpack. "But I'll be back. This isn't over."

"I didn't know you were moving in," Kyle mumbled, hiding behind the curtain.

I shoved two nights' worth of clothes and my notebook into my backpack, then went to the bathroom and added my comb and toothbrush to the mess. Pulling the drawstrings tight, I went back into my room and grabbed my purse, double-checking that my cigarettes, lighter, and wallet were still inside.

"See you soon, Kyle."

Kyle stared at me from his desk, not saying anything.

I stepped out of the house and into the yard. Everyone was in the same position, Dad on the stairs, Mom and the cop looming above him.

"That's all you're taking?" Mom said, pointing to my backpack.

"I'll come back for the rest later," I said, not moving toward the car.

"Fine. Get in." Mom got into her van, slammed the door shut, frowning at me, and grabbed the steering wheel in her hands.

"Thanks, Dad. Bye," I said.

"I'll call you later." Dad gave me a look that said, "I'm sorry about all this."

I smiled at him and got into the van.

The cop followed Mom's van out the driveway. Dad stayed on the stairs. He didn't wave.

Mom drove in silence, and for a while I pretended to be staring out the window, but my mind was racing, replaying what had just happened over and over in my head, trying to get a foothold. In less than twenty-four hours Mom had called the Ridge Meadows RCMP, arranged to pick me up with an accompanying officer, and showed up at Dad's house with scripted demands. She would have had Dad arrested, would have left Kyle at the house to fend for himself instead of letting us all be together. Anger welled as I realized she had only come for me, not for Kyle. Was I more valuable? Well behaved? Better suited to her new life? Why wouldn't she let me go?

I didn't know the answers, but I was sick of being at the mercy of two adults who treated their children like pawns to be moved about for tactical positioning and divorce proceedings. Dad's hands weren't clean, but at least he let me be who I needed to be. And it was Mom who had taken us from Nelson, Mom who had imposed a new living arrangement on us, Mom who had pushed Kyle out the door to make way for a set of strange children who I didn't know and didn't want to know. I couldn't go back, and knew that I had to think of something—fast.

"Mom, this isn't fair," I blurted out.

"Sure. Right. Fair," Mom huffed under her breath. She turned onto the highway toward Vancouver.

"You have to let me say goodbye to my friends. They all think I'm moving here."

"You can call them. From home."

I could tell it wasn't working and decided to switch gears.

"You can't do this to me again," I launched in. "You took me from Nelson, and I never got to say goodbye to anyone. Are you going to do that to me again?"

The words came out accusatory, an attempt to shame Mom into compliance.

"That's enough, Tanya," Mom cut me off. "Like I said, we can talk about it when we get home."

A frantic panic started to rise in me, the idea of getting on the ferry to Port Alberni making me feel faint.

"Look. Adam's place is ten minutes from here. Drop me off there for the rest of the weekend, and I'll come home Sunday."

"Forget it. That's a lie and you know it."

Jack shuffled around in his car seat, but he knew better than to say anything.

I leaned forward. I was running out of time. I needed to throw her own tactics back at her.

"If you don't drop me off right now, the next time you come to a stop sign, I will run out of the car and you'll never see me again."

My voice was deep, feigning confidence.

"Enough."

"You think I'm not serious? You think I won't?" I threatened.

Mom didn't answer.

"I will run away again and you'll never see me. It might happen here or it might happen in Port Alberni, but it will happen. And I won't run to Dad or to Stacy. I'll run where you'll never find me."

I clutched my backpack to my chest and undid my seatbelt.

"Drop me at Adam's and I'll come home Sunday. Don't drop me off and I'll run away. You know I can do it."

I was shaking. I wasn't sure if I could do it, but I felt like I could jump out of the moving car if I had to.

Mom heaved a breath and turned on her blinker. She pulled off the highway and took the underpass into the city.

"You better come back Sunday or there'll be hell to pay."

We navigated to Adam's through midday traffic, with the heat from the car exhaust rising off the pavement and through the open window. It was one of those summer days where the cement smelled like it was melting, a mix of asphalt and tar. I felt like I was hyperventilating. Anxiety buzzed inside my brain and my knees knocked up and down, bouncing my backpack on my lap like a fussy kid. They didn't stop knocking until I saw the cheap donut shop near Adam's place, and I knew we were only a couple of blocks away. I squeezed my bag against my chest, hoping that someone would be home.

"Do they know you're coming?"

"That was the plan," I lied.

"I'm going to wait," Mom said, pulling up in front of Adam's place.

"No, don't. They might be out, and I have a key."

Mom clutched the steering wheel.

"I have no idea why I'm letting you do this," she said.

"See you Sunday," I lied again.

I jumped out of the car and slammed the door. Mom rolled down the window.

"See you Sunday," Mom said, driving off without looking at me.

I didn't watch her drive away and instead ran toward the house, an oversized place with fading white shingles and the only uncut lawn on the block.

I ran around the back and knocked on the sliding glass door off the deck. Nothing. I looked inside the glass. The kitchen was a mess, plates and cups strewn all over the counter. This was a good sign. Someone had been there the night before. I knocked again, this time with a little more desperation.

Paul, Miranda's new boyfriend, came stumbling into the kitchen in his underwear and a faded white T-shirt.

"What the fuck," he said, opening the sliding glass door. "What are you doing here?"

I brushed past him into the house.

"Where's Miranda?" I asked.

"We're just waking up. Are you okay?"

"Where's Miranda?" I asked again.

"In here," I heard Miranda's voice from the bedroom.

There was no time for hellos. I tumbled into Miranda's room, where she was slipping into a black robe. I told them the situation and that I was running away.

"Don't try and stop me," I said. "I can't go back there."

Miranda reached out her hand. "Calm down, Tanya. No one's going to make you go anywhere," she said. She doled out cigarettes and put an ashtray on the bed. "I ran away when I was seventeen. Adam did too. That's how we ended up here. You can do it if you want to. You could stay here until you found a job, but it would be better to stay at your dad's."

"Yeah, at least at your dad's you could finish school. Unless you don't want to. Do you want to finish school?" Paul asked.

"It's the only way out of all this," I said. "It's the only thing I know for sure."

"At least then you could go to college. Once you're in school you can move out, get a student loan, move into the city. It's only a year away."

"And then we'll be so close," Miranda added. "Isn't there a way you could do that?

"I don't know. They were going to arrest my dad today. Can you believe that?"

Paul's eyes widened a little.

"I think you should at least call your dad and tell him where you are," he suggested.

"He's probably really worried," Miranda chimed in.

I hadn't thought that far ahead, but they were right. Dad had been left on his front stoop, and I could see him sitting there still, slack jawed and wondering what had just happened.

"Can I make the call in here?" I asked.

Both Miranda and Paul nodded. "We'll be in the kitchen. We were about to make coffee anyway."

Miranda handed me the phone and they left. I dialed the number and Dad picked up right away.

"Dad?"

"Tanya, where are you?" he blurted out, almost overlapping me.

I explained the drive with Mom, my ultimatum, and how I got to Adam and Miranda's.

"I want you to call my lawyer. You need to call him and tell him what happened today. I just talked to him and your mother can't arrest me. He's a good guy. He's on our side."

"Okay," I said, pulling a pen out of my purse and writing the number on my hand.

"Get his advice and then call me back," Dad said and hung up.

I dialed the number for Dad's lawyer and he picked up right away.

"Hello, your dad mentioned you might call. I just spoke with him. Where are you?"

I told my story again, trying to sound professional as I told it.

"I see," the lawyer said.

"Can you advise me?"

"Legally, I can't officially advise you because you aren't my client, but I can provide you with information on behalf of your father. You would assume any legal responsibility for yourself. I couldn't represent you in this matter as it would be a conflict of interest, given that I represent your father. And none of this advice should replace your own legal counsel or stand up in court."

"Yeah, of course," I said, not knowing what I was agreeing to.

"You're sixteen?"

"Almost seventeen."

"At sixteen, under current law, you are technically an adult. As an adult, you have the right to choose for yourself where you live and how you choose to live. Your parents have no jurisdiction over you. Legally," the lawyer emphasized.

"So if my mother came to take me from my father, that would be illegal?"

"You would be under no legal obligation to go with her, nor could she arrest your father. If you chose, you could file to become a ward of the state. Then neither parent would legally be responsible for you. And if she harassed you, you could file a restraining order, or sue her for harassment."

"I could sue her."

"If you felt you had the grounds, yes."

"I don't have to live with her if I don't want to."

"Legally, no."

"Great, that's all I wanted to know. Thanks."

My heart was pounding furiously as I hung up the phone and dialed Dad.

"Call your mother tonight and tell her what you know. I'll see you Sunday. Great work," Dad said.

There was no time to think and so there was no time to second-guess what Dad meant when he said, "Great work," no time to know that I was about to do my father's bidding by making my own mother feel powerless, no time to see how little I would thrive in Dad's household, parentless and watching Dad drink himself into full-blown oblivion. There was no time for all that, and even if there had been, I still wouldn't have gone back to Port Alberni. All I knew was that I wanted to be with my friends, where I felt strong and loved. Dad was rudderless, and I didn't want a rudder. I wanted to be left alone.

"Hello, Mother."

There was a silence on her end, but I knew it was her.

"Mother, I want you to listen very closely. I've called a lawyer and I know my rights."

I heard a hefty sigh from her end.

"Legally, I am an adult. You cannot force me to live anywhere I don't want to live, and you cannot come and forcibly remove me from wherever I choose to live. If you try and stop me from living at Dad's, I will sue you for harassment, and if you push me, I will become a ward of the state and get a restraining order. Do you understand?"

"Tanya . . ."

"No. This shit is done. Do you understand? It's over. Do you understand?"

There was a heavy silence.

"Yes," Mom said. "Yes, I understand."

"Good."

I hung up the phone. It was over. And I was so happy that I immediately went out that night with Miranda and got blackout drunk.

Buried

My bed at Dad's was a twin-sized mattress on the floor, with a nightstand that I made out of two cardboard boxes stacked one inside the other and covered with an old sheet from Dad's linen closet. On top of the nightstand were my pack of Du Mauriers, a lighter, and a small glass ashtray. I had taken the ashtray from Dad's special cupboard where he kept the ashtrays next to the beer mugs and shot glasses he collected from the liquor stores he visited, each one etched with the logos of his favorite brands.

Most days Dad would get up at dawn. His coughing would wake me up, and I would hear him walking down the hallway. A few minutes later, the smell of his cigarette wafting down the hall would cue me to roll onto my side and light up. I liked to smoke the first cigarette of the day lying down, my nervous system zigzagging and my taste buds crying out for that first drag. I'd flip open the cardboard flap of my pack and with a crinkling sound fold my fingers around the filter of a cigarette to pull it out and light up. My morning cigarette was heaven on earth. Every time. By the time I butted it out, I would be sitting propped up against the wall with a couple of pillows.

Picking out the right clothes was an art form, one I didn't take lightly. My eyes would wander through my closet, where clothes hung by shade from black to gray to white. I owned three pairs of shoes—black Converse, a pair of scuffed black ankle boots, and my own pair of twenty-hole steel-toe boots. My favorite outfit was a black velvet skirt, a man's white button-up shirt, fishnets, and my steel toes. I would pair this outfit with the chain-mail collar and chain-mail garters Lana made for me, but I would wear the garters on the outside of the skirt, where they could clang against my thighs and be seen by everybody at Maple Ridge Secondary, where I had started two weeks after my run-in with Mom and the police.

I had adjusted to my new school the same way I had adjusted to every other school my parents had dragged me to throughout my childhood, and quickly made friends with the outcasts. We smoked cigarettes together and spent the occasional weekend at a party, but my senior year wasn't about school so much as what was beyond it—college and getting to Vancouver, where I saw my life beginning to unfold.

Dad packed our lunches and made our dinners. It was one of the parental things he could manage. For a while we had a vacuum sealer, a rectangular machine that sucked the air out of plastic bags so that you could freeze leftovers and prepackage nuts. Dad was obsessed with it, and bought dollar bags of Jujubes, peanuts, and beef jerky to vacu-suck them into individual portions for our lunches.

A couple of months after moving in with Dad, I was invited to sit with some of Kyle's friends in the school hallway by an older goth kid who was into WWF wrestling and Marilyn Manson. He didn't know I was Kyle's sister, and when I sat down, Kyle shot me a look that said, "You can sit here, but don't say we're related."

Fair enough, I thought, assuming there was some kind of pecking order in their group that I didn't fully understand. Chatting, we opened our puddings and sandwiches and carrot sticks. I ripped open a Vacupack of Jujubes and started eating.

"Hey, Kyle, doesn't your Dad Vacupack your lunch too?" the goth kid observed.

Kyle and I looked at each other and burst out laughing.

"He's my brother," I said.

Everyone looked confused.

"We're brother and sister," I repeated.

There was a pause while everyone registered the information and then there was laughter. Kyle and I looked at each other again, but this time, we were relieved.

Dad would have his first beer around noon. Kokanee was his beer of choice, but if his work was slow, there would be empty cans of generic beer next to the sink that he would recycle for money at the end of the month, when he needed it to buy more beer. He would drink four or five beers right away, sipping the first two and guzzling the rest. On a school day we would come home as Dad was beginning to ride a buzz. If it was a weekend, we would watch Dad get drunk, and he would make us get him one beer after another from the fridge while he worked on vacuums in the garage.

He could always manage dinner. We would have great family meals, roast beef and potatoes, seafood chowder, homemade pizza subs. That was the climax of his day. With his fatherly duty done, he could switch to vodka.

Mostly Dad mixed his own drinks, but sometimes he would get me to mix drinks for him. When he was at the point where he couldn't mix his own drinks, he was a mean, loud drunk. When he got this way, I had to be nice and hope that he would make it through dinner and then pass out in the living room with a full drink getting tepid on a coaster beside him.

Kyle and I could clock Dad's state of mind during dinner, exchanging quick side glances, jumping to grab a salt shaker before it spilled or sweeping an arm under the table to grab the fork before it hit the floor. I would clean the dishes while Kyle and Dad sat at the table, and then, if Dad wasn't too smashed, we would watch movies together.

We watched comedies. Anything to make us laugh and especially anything that would make Dad laugh. It was hard to get him to laugh, sitting in his chair with the lights glistening off his watery eyes. He wasn't an easy sell. But when he did laugh it was genuine, and then Kyle and I would laugh at his laughing, and we would all have a moment to breathe.

Bill Murray was far and away the family favorite. We had *What About Bob?*, *Groundhog Day*, and *Ghostbusters,* but nothing could top *Scrooged,* which could bring all of us to tears, laughing so loud that we drowned out the dialogue. We watched it every Christmas.

Visiting Dad the year after the divorce, he made a fuss over putting up the Christmas tree.

"Fuck this, you guys. No movies, no presents, no fucking tree. Christmas is bullshit. We're gonna sit around like any other day, sit in our pajamas and sleep in."

"But Dad, we always put up the Christmas tree. That's the rule. It's tradition. We have to do it," I said.

"I'm not going to do shit," he grumbled.

I watched him retreat into his chair and could see the next hellish month beginning to reveal itself. Listening to the sound of a vodka bottle being uncorked at eight o'clock in the morning. Temper tantrums because of lost keys. Slurred words that I would have to pretend to understand.

"Where do you store the tree?" I asked.

Dad said nothing.

"Kyle, pull up some Christmas music on your computer. Bring the speakers from your room."

Kyle ran off down the hall.

"Dad, you don't have to do anything. I'll take care of it."

Dad's cold stare seemed unbreakable.

"Where is the tree?" I asked again.

"Crawl space," Dad barked.

I went to the hallway closet and dragged out the old ornaments. By the time I had gotten back, Nat King Cole was playing over Kyle's computer speakers, and he was staring at me, begging for a task.

"Start unraveling these," I said, pressing the ball of Christmas lights to Kyle's gut.

Already half-drunk, Dad tried to get out of his chair, when the glass tumbler in his hand started to fall.

"Dad." I quickly stepped toward him, and he fell backward into his La-Z-Boy. "Just sit here. Let us do it."

When I climbed into the crawl space under the cement stairs that led to our front door, I had to squeeze my body under the house and reach blindly with my hand to feel around in the darkness. There was a light frost on the ground and I thought I might slip, but eventually I felt a damp cardboard box and inched it toward me. It was heavy, and I had to pull at it because the cardboard kept crumbling off in my hands. When I finally got it out from under the house, I saw that the box was long and small, with mold along its edges. I opened it to make sure I had grabbed the right box, and there it was, just like I remembered. A tiny, fake, toxic Christmas tree, broken into color-coded branches, ready to be reassembled.

Dad was still in his chair when I ran back into the house. For the rest of the night, I acted as coach, yelling out commands and doling out encouragement. "Put the tinsel here," I said, pointing at the top branch, or "That looks good Kyle, it's almost there, just pull the bottom branches apart a bit more so that it won't look so fake."

After an hour, we got the tree set up in the nook between the hall-way and the dining room.

"The lights blink." Dad suddenly rose from his chair. "They blink and sing Christmas songs."

Kyle turned his computer off. We all took a breath, and I motioned for Kyle to turn out the lights. Then I plugged in the tree. Blues, reds, greens, and yellows all started blinking in rhythm to "Silent Night." We

watched. We watched for a long time, listening to the tinkling *bling,*
bling, bling of the spiritual hymn, calling us to be peaceful and calm.

In Dad's living room, often after midnight, he would confess to me
while drinking himself into a blackout. About how lonely he was, about
what a cunt my mother was, about what it was like to have sex with her,
about what she liked to do, about what he would do to her, what he was
allowed to do, what he wasn't allowed to do, about what he would have
liked to do, about what all men like to do, and what they need you to do
to them, and how to do those things. He would describe them in detail.

"I'm telling you this so you won't be like your mother. You know
that," Dad would mumble. "You gotta be a good girlfriend."

I would sit and stare past him, through his face and the smoke and
the stinking carpet. I would try not to listen. I would try not to imagine
what he was describing but felt I had to endure it. It never occurred to
me that I could leave.

When I think of those moments now, I feel all the things a grown
woman is supposed to feel—anger, hatred, disgust, a desire to help
other young women understand self-respect and to educate boys about
respecting women. But back then, all I knew was survival. When you're
just thinking about surviving, when you've been abused and berated,
hurt as a child before you even had the language to describe the hurt
like I had, you come to believe that the world is a traumatic place, without respite. Holding someone's hand doesn't just scare you—it makes
you feel like cutting it off. And that's when you know you're in a lot of
trouble.

And even after years of struggling, after dropping the alcohol and
the cigarettes and the sex, after therapy and silent retreats, yoga classes
and acupuncture and Rolfing, prayer and meditation, the trying and
failing and trying again to learn how to give and receive love, I have

to trust in my own strength and all the work that I've done to parent myself. Because I also know how little it takes to break a broken person.

At the local art supply store, they always had unlined hardcover sketchbooks on sale. I would get one every month because it could easily fit into my backpack, and by month's end it would be full.

I filled the sketchbooks with writing—working out poems, sometimes letting them spill out across two or more pages, madly writing diagonally, horizontally, and vertically. Once I had a poem, I would cut pictures out of magazines and let the images behave like the poems, overlapping cutouts in all directions until a chaotic form emerged, eyeballs and words glued on top of black-and-white photographs, postcards, leaves I had found on the ground, dried flowers, and drawings of faceless women. Alongside these strange collages I would try a second poem, one with a more traditional structure, sonnets or haikus, trying, always trying, to make something out of the madness.

On the inside covers I copied quotes from Shakespeare, Bram Stoker's *Dracula*, David Wojnarowicz, and the lyrics to King Missile's "Detachable Penis." Being left-handed, I wrote from the back of the book to the front, my hand scuffing across the page like a clubfoot. Because I only used BIC pens, the blue ink always stained the side of my left hand. The only time it was clean was after a bath, but it wouldn't last long. I would go charging into my room so that I could write down all the thoughts that had come to me in the bathroom, the ink seeping into my skin, marking my flesh.

One morning, riding the bus to Vancouver for the weekend, we came to a stop along Hastings Street. An old woman in a flower-print dress was leaning out of her window on the top floor of a brick apartment building. A wrought-iron fire escape zigzagged along the outside, and it reminded me of the game Snakes and Ladders. The old woman was smoking a rolled cigarette, her back curved against the window frame, her large thigh bracing her from falling out onto the fire escape. Her face looked ravaged—pockmarked, with dark eyes and swarthy skin. She was looking down at the scene below: the public bus, the crack addicts whirling along the crowded street, and the dirty-faced punk kids begging for a little coin, watching the steam from the chicken joint on Cordova wafting toward the bus and reading the sign out front, "10 pieces for 5 bucks."

The image was raw, uninhibited, and grotesque. It touched my heart. I felt as ravaged as the old woman, my thoughts and feelings unsettled and swerving around me. To me, I was looking at life. Boiling, pus-filled, oozing. It had the stink of rotten chicken and piss and I inhaled it deeply.

I am alive, I kept repeating to myself, kept writing in my diary. *I am alive, I am alive, I am alive.*

Fool for Love

Every day that I walked to Maple Ridge Secondary, I spoke *Hamlet.* It was my secret language, the iambic pentameter influencing my steps, the cars honking when they passed me because there was no sidewalk. When they drove by, I would step into the grass and stare into a creek that ran alongside the road. It was filled with soda cans and McDonald's wrappers, and I was so devoted to memorizing Hamlet's soliloquies that I felt a poetic connection between the text and the garbage below.

Halfway through twelfth grade, I took a directing class where each student had to direct a show and act in one of the other directors' shows. I decided to direct Anton Chekhov's *The Proposal.* We had an open casting call, and since I had cast landowner Stepan Stepanovitch Chubukov and his daughter, Natalya Stepanovna, using fellow directing students, all I needed to cast was Natalya's young male suitor, landowner and neighbor Ivan Vassilevitch Lomov. Most of the boys who came to the open call weren't able to handle Chekhov's text, but one kid, Mike, totally blew me away. At least he could pronounce the larger words without stumbling.

After I cast him, one of the directors told me Mike was a recovering drug addict on probation. Curious and a bit worried for the other actors, I walked Mike home after rehearsal one day to talk about it.

"What did you get arrested for?" I asked him.

"Drug possession. I wasn't selling at the time, I just had it on me and someone busted me. One morning I woke up with a boot on my face. This cop said, 'Don't move, Mike. We found you, motherfucker.'

I got probation for being a minor. One year and then I'll be free and clear."

Mike found it impossible to show up to rehearsals on time, even though they took place during school hours. I would have to go find him. He was either smoking in the back alley or walking up and down the hallways.

"Mike, come on, man."

"Ah, fuck, you found me," he would always say in mock anger.

Mike was terrified by the idea of having to memorize his lines. This made him sweaty, frustrated, and nervous, which was perfect for the character, but it filled Mike with anxiety.

"I've never done anything like this before. I can't memorize all this shit. It's impossible."

"Listen, Mike, if you do this, I will buy you a forty pounder of any kind of booze you want. No questions asked. A whole forty."

"You serious?" Mike asked.

"Yeah. I'll throw in a pack of smokes too, if you're interested."

"Just for being in the play?"

"Just for being in the play."

Mike couldn't see what I saw. When he was onstage he was completely present. He had no idea what he was doing and all he could do was react—which made him mesmerizing.

The day before the show Mike went MIA. I couldn't find him in any of his old haunts and thought we were screwed until he walked in right before our tech rehearsal.

"I told myself I wasn't going to come here," Mike said. "I can't do this. Why'd you give me the part anyway?"

"Because you're awesome," I said. "You're one of the best actors I've seen. And if you don't think you can memorize your lines, you can do the show with the script in your hand. I just think you're perfect for it is all."

"You do?" Mike asked.

"Yeah."

"Yeah, Mike, let's do this. It'll be fun," Stepan Stepanovitch Chubukov said in his white cravat and brown oxford shoes.

Natalya nodded in agreement. "Oh yes, Mike, let's do it."

"You guys want me to do this thing?"

"Fuck yeah!" we all yelled.

"All right," Mike said, "but I still get my booze."

"It's a deal, motherfucker. Now get backstage and try on your pleated cummerbund. We are going to rock this bitch."

And he rocked it. No book in hand, Mike showed up the next day, lines memorized, and we had a great time. And I did buy him the booze. He earned it.

Near the end of twelfth grade, my creative writing teacher wanted to take us to a piece of interactive dinner theater called *Tony n' Tina's Wedding*. My father refused to pay the ten-dollar ticket fee.

"It's public school for fuck's sake. Public means free. Anything that isn't free isn't public."

Later that year he used the same excuse when I brought home the invoice for my school photos. I would have been upset if it mattered. *It doesn't*, I told myself. *I am going to be in theater school in the fall. I am going to move out and be in plays about families and never have to see my family again.*

"We'll come out and get you when we're ready."

No one drove me, but I didn't care. I was sitting on a red plastic office chair in a dark hallway next to a set of black double doors, and I had taken the bus by myself, two and a half hours from Maple Ridge to North Vancouver.

Capilano College sent a notification letter with my audition time, when I would perform two monologues and take part in a group exercise. The group had met earlier that morning, and I was nervous but thought it went well. Amy, the musical theater teacher, led a vocal warm-up, and Andy and Ron, the directing and acting teachers, led a few physical exercises. I stood in a circle and tried to stay open to the other actors. We were all young and overeager. At the end of the group audition, Andy thanked everyone and posted our half-hour audition slots.

"Feel free to explore the campus while you're waiting," Andy encouraged us.

I had never been to a college before and didn't know anything about it. Mom graduated high school but never made it to college. Instead she got pregnant with me. Dad never graduated from high school. I applied to the college because they had a theater program—no other reason. I didn't know that when you apply to college, you are supposed to do your research and find the college that has the best reputation and the highest number of employable graduates. I just wanted to make theater with people who made theater. I had no idea what I was getting into, but the campus was beautiful and tucked away in the forests of North Vancouver.

Andy had told us that the theater was in the main building, and I wanted to see it, so I walked down paths surrounded by trees, diligently following the signs, trying not to get lost. The campus was immaculately clean and smelled like wet leaves. As the path opened up, I saw the library, a small building with windows looking in on rows of books. A few students were standing outside, studying at benches or standing around with their friends.

The main building was a large glass tower looming above a sea of expensive-looking cars. Inside the building was a cafeteria, and I noticed how preened the students looked, with their well-kept hair and Tommy Hilfiger jackets. I was wearing the goth attire I'd bought from a thrift store, a man's secondhand work shirt, black jeans with a ripped back-pack, and black Converse with holes in the toes.

The thing was, I didn't care. *If I get in,* I told myself, *I'll be too busy to care.*

"Tanya?"

Andy opened the door to the theater, and I quickly gathered my things.

I walked into a small rehearsal hall. The walls, ceiling, and floors were all black, and three rows of theater lights lit up the space. Andy took a seat behind a table next to Ron and Amy.

"So," Andy said, moving a few papers around, "what will you be showing us today?"

"I've prepared a monologue from Sam Shepard's *Fool for Love.* I'll be playing May."

Ron perked up.

"I love Sam Shepard. Great choice."

I shuffled my feet and smiled, happy I had pleased one of the teachers.

"Please," Ron said, "whenever you're ready."

I had been reading the play for weeks. At night I rehearsed in my room and planned everything. How I would enter, where I would stand, when I would emphasize a certain word, the tilt of my head, the running tableau of pictures I would see in my mind.

I took a breath and I spoke. I put myself in May's world, a world of longing for the father who had abandoned her, a world of anger for her brother-lover, Eddie. How Eddie's mother had shot herself after her father left, and how May and Eddie had clung to each other until it had all gone horribly wrong, as things tend to in Shepard's plays, and how May tried to escape the strange love affair that she found herself in.

It felt good to speak out loud, not whisper the words in my bedroom, and I could feel the power of the words as I was saying them, coming off the page and out into space. After I was done, Andy, Ron, and Amy thanked me and invited me to sit in front of the table. I grabbed a chair and sat down.

"Thank you," Ron said. "Shepard is so dark. I love him."

"Thank you," I said, unsure of the right response.

They asked me a few questions about high school, and I told them about directing Chekhov. Then Andy went into a rehearsed speech.

"We like to tell the students a bit about what it's like in the program," he said, "just to give them an idea of what to expect."

I sat up in my seat.

"In the first year, students do studio work in the mornings, theater history classes, voice, and acting. They take technical theater classes and an improv class in the spring. All first-year students are on the tech crew for the mainstage productions. So there are a lot of late nights."

I nodded.

"Then in the second year, students who choose to stay in the acting stream perform in the mainstage shows. Sometimes students discover that after the first year they want to switch to the technical stream, and those students learn design and stage management. Eventually they either design or stage-manage a mainstage show alongside a professional director."

"Well, I definitely want to act," I blurted out, "I know that. I need to learn how to act. That's what I want to do."

The teachers shared side-glances.

"That's good that you know what you want," Andy said. "That's a wonderful thing."

I nodded again.

"Do you have any questions for us?" Amy asked.

"When will we know if we got into the program?"

"In about a month. Then you have to register and fill out forms, pay your tuition, and that's that."

"Great," I said with naïve confidence. "I'll be applying for student loans so that will give me time to find a place to live."

I could see that the teachers were surprised—I hadn't been accepted yet.

"Good, good," Andy said. "You'll hear from us in about a month."

Neon

Soft light poured into my bedroom, and I lay in it for a while, feeling the weight of the blankets against my body. It was six a.m. on graduation day, the last day of an old life and the first day of a new one. I wanted to sit in the space between them for a moment, still and breathing.

I missed Mom. She would be at the ceremony by herself, without children, husbands, or distractions. It seemed right that she would come alone. I was the oldest child, and I remembered her when she was almost my age.

When I was three, Mom and I lived in a dilapidated house in a rough neighborhood in Regina, Saskatchewan. On weekends she would watch me spinning round and round like a Sufi, spinning in the open space between the living room and the kitchen for hours. Her hair ran all the way past the belt loops of her jeans, long, thin, and easily mismanaged. I would try and run my hands through her hair and get my fingers tangled up in it. Mom would have to pull at the hair wrapped around my chubby fingers, which was cutting off my circulation and making them look like tiny red sausages.

One night Mom had a few extra dollars from her retail job at Sears. She took me to the corner store and told me to wait inside the car while she went to get a pack of smokes. I watched her through the window, and it seemed to me as if she were a creature from another planet, crossing the threshold of the doorway into neon light. Walking past the magazine rack, Mom leaned over and grabbed something. I couldn't see what it was. Smiling, she turned and pressed the object against the store window. I squinted, leaning forward, and took a long look, my legs dangling off the car seat, my fingers barely able to touch the dashboard.

It was a book. Mom mouthed the words, "Want it?" I clapped my hands and mouthed back, "Yes."

When Mom came back to the car, she read the title before passing the book back to me.

"*Heidi*. This book is called *Heidi* and it's about a little girl your age."

My small knuckles ached from holding the book all the way home. Mom read it to me over and over, and that night we slept side by side in her room, dreaming of the Swiss Alps and a little girl with two perfect braids.

"No matter what, we're going to make it through, sweetheart. We're tough, we're Hungarian. Magyar."

We came from Hungarian farmers, and if we went further back, there were rumors of Gypsy blood. And since we always had it tough, Mom knew we'd always make it through as long as we had each other.

"No one loves you like I love you," she would say to me.

I remember Mom teaching me how to cut out snowflakes.

"Let me show you something," she said, getting up from her place at the kitchen table.

She came back with a pair of scissors and an old newspaper.

"That's no fun." I pushed the paper away.

"When you don't have a lot, you learn to make fun where you can find it, honey," Mom said, "because then it's magic. It's like a secret no one knows but you."

I huffed a child's huff, and Mom unfolded a piece of the newsprint and then ripped it in half.

"Now look here," she whispered, almost to herself.

She laid the newsprint down on the table and folded it in half a few times to make a tiny square.

"See how small it is?" she asked. "Now, pass me the scissors."

I carefully passed her the scissors the way she had taught me, holding the sharp end instead of the handle.

Mom cut half circles and tiny hearts along the paper's edge, and then she held the square in one hand and folded it at its middle to cut out two diamonds, like she was cutting into a fat chunk of meat.

Mom put the scissors down and held up the square.

"What do you think will happen if I open this square, sweetheart?"

"Mommy, it's just gonna fall apart. You've cut it all up."

"No, honey. I just made a snowflake."

"No, you didn't." I leaned forward.

"I did. I did," Mom said.

And she pulled at the edges of the square, giving them a gentle tug. The square unfurled, expanding into a strange black-and-white snowflake made of diamonds, circles, and half moons.

Mom was twenty-three when she made me that snowflake. I was only six.

I didn't care that we were poor, although I didn't understand what being poor meant until I went to kindergarten and met kids from other walks of life. But by then my new dad was around and he was making money. By kindergarten I had new shoes and My Little Ponies and Cabbage Patch Kids.

Mom had been pregnant with me when she was seventeen, the same age I was. I tried to imagine my biological father. I wondered if he knew my age and that I was graduating. I didn't have a clue where he was, and though part of me had wanted to, I had never asked my mom to find him. She told me that he had broken her heart, and that feeling—loving someone who doesn't love you—was the worst feeling in the world. Sometimes I liked to imagine how they met, my mother a young woman strolling down a sidewalk, a beautiful young man walking down the same sidewalk in the opposite direction. Maybe they saw one another, or maybe they slammed into one another, their scents commingling as they balanced, precariously, in an accidental midair embrace before they tripped and fell to the ground. But it was my imagination, a strange thought, and I rolled over in bed to escape it.

My closet door was closed but inside was my prom dress, custom made by Krista, a part-time seamstress and exotic belly dancer. She had measured me for the dress at her place downtown.

"You're a tiny thing for being so tall," Krista said, wrapping me with sheets and pinning me into place.

"Do you think you can still make me a dress that will fit? With me being so small and everything?"

"Honey, calm down. It's an observation, not a judgment."

"Oh," I said, trying not to fidget.

"Don't move." Krista plunged a needle into the fabric under my ribcage. "You even breathe funny and this thing's gonna pop."

After Krista unwrapped me, I changed and then came back to her in the kitchen. She was scribbling on a notepad.

"I made some tea," she said.

I poured some into two cups and brought them to the table. Krista pushed the notepad toward me.

"How about this?"

I looked down and saw my prom dress, the same prom dress that was hanging in my closet a month later, the same prom dress from her original drawing. It was made from black PVC, sewn into two long pieces that fit snug around my ribs and upper torso and hung down to the floor. It hooked at the nape of my neck with a small silver clasp and two slits cut up the side of my legs, showing off my twenty-holed steel toes, fishnets, and upper thighs. Krista had also measured my hands and surprised me with a set of matching PVC gloves.

"The gloves are on the house," she said. "Apparently you only go to prom once."

Dad was making morning coffee in the kitchen. Above the fridge was the acceptance letter to college. When it had come, I had felt it all over, the thickness of the envelope heavy in my hands. In the fall, I would leave home. I was going to theater school.

Later that night, Lana, Garret, and Adam would take me to the Twilight Zone. At the end of Adam's set, he would play my favorite Björk song, "Hyperballad," as I walked out onto the dance floor, the strobe lights flashing across my face. Björk's voice would wash over me, and I would tilt my head back and open my mouth, curling upward in absolute joy, the way a turtle opens its mouth to gulp up the rain, drowning in the ecstasy of sensation.

But first, graduation. I rubbed my face into my pillows, feeling the fuzzy old cotton against my face. The sun had warmed me to waking. It was time to get up.

ACKNOWLEDGMENTS

Parts of this book have appeared in many forms, from theater to radio to literary publication, and I would like to thank Abby Wendle and NPR's *Invisibilia,* Neon Signs, the PuSh Festival, Theatre Conspiracy, the Brooklyn Arts Exchange, The Tank, Playwrights Theatre Centre, Proximity Arts, Mabou Mines, and the Collapsable Hole for giving me space to tell my story. I am forever grateful.

Special thanks to my agent, Erin Hosier, for her fierce encouragement, and to Carmen Johnson, whose insight and editorial ability to see what is hidden beneath the surface is astounding. My writing and the book are better for all that you do. Thanks to everyone at Little A, whose support allowed me to focus on my writing, and to Ian Poole, Selean Kitchen, and Mom for the photographs.

There were many readers who gave me inspiration and invaluable feedback, including Heidi Taylor, Adrienne Wong, Gabe Kruis, Miranda Huba, Ryan Daniel-Healy, Jay Scouten, Ilena Lee Cramer, Sherry and Laura Killam, Jason McNair, Su-Feh Lee, DD Kugler, Michele Valiquette, Nneka and Aida Croal, Tim Carlson, Mallory Catlett, Jon Wood, Ed Gooding, Jaime Wolf, Emily Reilly, Norman Armour, my cohort in the MFA Creative Writing Program at Hunter College, and my writing and theater students, who keep me connected, however remotely, to the sixteen-year-old kid inside me.

To my mentors, Kathryn Harrison, Louise DeSalvo, and Alexandra Styron, who kept pushing me and who believed in me even when I couldn't, or wouldn't, or didn't. None of this would have been possible without your guidance.

To the healing that this book brought to my relationship with my mother. To my brothers for their memories and for bearing witness. To my stepbrothers and stepsister, and to my family in Winnipeg—some family we know from birth, and some become our family later. I hold you all in my heart.

And to my darling David B. Smith, who shows me the tenderest parts of love.

ABOUT THE AUTHOR

Photo © 2016 David B. Smith

Tanya Marquardt is an award-winning performer and the author of ten plays, which have been produced across Canada and the United States. *Transmission* was published in the *Canadian Theatre Review*, and *Some Must Watch While Some Must Sleep* was the subject of an episode of NPR's *Invisibilia*. A Hertog Fellow and graduate of the MFA creative writing program at Hunter College, Tanya splits her time between Vancouver, British Columbia, and Brooklyn, New York. *Stray* is her first book.